ONLY THE BEST

By the same author

EYE OF THE STORM
ABORTION: A WOMAN'S BIRTHRIGHT?

ONLY THE BEST

Noreen Riols

HODDER AND STOUGHTON
LONDON SYDNEY AUCKLAND TORONTO

British Library Cataloguing in Publication Data

Riols, Noreen.
  Only the best.—(Hodder Christian paper-
  back)
  1. Christian life
  I. Title
  248.4   BV4501.2

ISBN 0 340 40898 7

Hodder and Stoughton Editorial Office: 47 Bedford Square, London WC1B 3DP

TO

MY FAMILY

Homes are made by the wisdom of women.
Proverbs 14:1 (*Good News Bible*)

CONTENTS

INTRODUCTION

When the chambermaid entered a hotel room one morning to clean it she noticed a Gideon Bible open on the bedside table, and on picking it up, she realised that a message had been written on the inside of the back cover. It was addressed to 'whom it may concern' and read as follows:

'I rented this room with the thought of killing myself. This Bible saved my life. Proverbs 14: 1. "Homes are made by the wisdom of women, but are destroyed by foolishness." (Good News Bible).' It was signed 'Grateful' and after the signature she had added: 'This book is blessed.'

That testimony touched me deeply when I heard it and I marvelled yet again at the power of God's Word, which can save us spiritually and emotionally as well as physically, as in this desperate case. I was also intrigued by the proverb which this woman had read 'by chance' – a chance lovingly planned by God.

As I opened my Bible to read it I immediately understood why those few words had so dramatically changed her determination to end her life. And it is this proverb which I chose to accompany the dedication to my book.

It reminds us that a woman as a wife and mother really is the hub of the family wheel. On her depends the harmony, the happiness and the cohesion of those most dear to her, her husband and her children. The 'wise' mother also has a tremendous influence on her growing family as she helps to shape the thought patterns of her children and moulds the soft, impressionable clay of their minds. Because of the seeds she sows, together with her husband, during those formative years by her words, positive or negative, her actions, good or bad, by the example she gives to her children, and the principles she instils into them, she is directly affecting the future behaviour and upbringing not only of her own children but of the next generation as her grandchildren's and even her great-grandchildren's lives will be affected.

Remembering my own childhood, I realised the influence the different members of my family had on me during my formative years. In these pages, through which I have traced a thread spanning well over 130 years from my Victorian grandmother to the present day, I recall how this influence is felt for even three generations and beyond, and how a chance remark which my mother didn't even realise I had heard not only helped me as a child, but also came back to my mind to comfort and encourage me during troubled times.

In this book I have also tried to show the importance of a loving family, an extended family, embracing not only parents, brothers and sisters, but stretching beyond to the security which a solid background of grandparents, uncles, aunts and cousins can give to the growing child. The sense of warmth and security which their presence gave me during my growing years provided the springboard from which I was able to launch myself confidently into adult life.

When I married and chose to be 'just a housewife', fewer women worked after marriage so I did not feel guilty about staying at home. But today many women who decide temporarily to abandon their career and devote themselves entirely to their families, at least until the children are old enough to fend for themselves, do often have a complex about being 'just a housewife'. This sense of guilt is vigorously fanned by the media.

As I look back on my life, I realise that being a parent carries with it an enormous responsibility which, during the early formative years of a child's life, falls mostly on the mother who stays at home. Being a full-time wife and mother is a career and a very demanding one, requiring not only patience, strength, intelligence, tact and time but many other qualifications as well.

But how quickly their childhood passes, never to return, and compared with our life expectancy, what a short span of time we are actually 'tied down with the children'. And I know that those years when I was the hub of the family wheel were worth it. But the difference, the turning point in my attitude to this all-important task, which brought me peace and joy and satisfaction in the midst of everyday monotony, came when I met Jesus Christ as my personal Saviour and placed my life, my tiredness, my fears and my problems, and those of my growing family, into his hands.

It was only then that I realised that even if the world and the media consider women who have chosen the old-fashioned role to be second-class citizens, the one person whose opinion is really of value, our Lord Jesus, most certainly does not.

Noreen Riols
Marly-le-Roi

January 1987

Chapter 1

A CHANCE REMARK

'It's really not worth using grandmother's tea service today Nora,' Sybil said tartly, 'we're only family.'

There was a moment's tense silence as my mother and her cousin faced each other across the tea trolley. Then my mother smiled and, turning back to the sideboard, carefully took down the rest of the delicate china and placed it on the tray.

'My family are my most important guests,' she answered quietly.

I looked up from the hearthrug where I was sitting cross-legged in front of the flickering fire, holding a crumpet on a long-handled brass fork out to the blaze. My mother's words had strangely moved me, and I was never to forget them.

'Oh Nora, you and your kids,' Sybil snorted disgustedly, as she began arranging the pretty blue and gold cups on the tray. 'They'll end up by breaking them.'

And then she added a parting shot.

'I never did understand why grandfather left them to you!'

But my mother only smiled as she turned to go back to the kitchen where the kettle was whistling that it had reached boiling point.

Sybil and her biting tongue always frightened me. But at that moment I felt a deep resentment well up in me against this bossy middle-aged relative, who strongly disapproved of the lax discipline in our home and always seemed to take over whenever she came to stay, frequently quoting her Victorian theory that 'children should be seen but not heard'.

'She's the one who'll end up breaking them,' I muttered to myself as I watched her, in her annoyance, handling the cups with less care than usual.

'Sybil,' my mother said patiently, as she placed the teapot on the tray, 'those cups have been used by dozens of children. We used them, our mothers did...'

'Children were different in those days,' Sybil cut in, angry at not getting her own way.

'That's what every generation says,' my mother answered smoothly. 'It's a sign that we're getting old.'

Sybil sniffed and pushed the trolley across the hall and into the drawing room.

My mother stooped to pick up the plate with the growing pile of toasted crumpets on the floor beside me.

'Don't worry about Sybil,' she whispered, 'her bark is worse than her bite.'

'I don't think she likes children,' I whispered back.

My mother knelt down beside me, looking into the fire.

'Don't think that,' she said softly. 'If ever you're in trouble...'

She paused, maybe her thoughts were going ahead to the coming war, to the ever increasing rumbles which grown-ups heard but of which we children were blissfully unaware. This was the last Sunday in 1938; the last Christmas holiday before the world was to be torn apart by World War Two.

My mother looked straight at me.

'You can always rely on Sybil,' she ended. 'She may not appear to be interested in you but, deep down, she loves you dearly and I know she'd do anything for either of you.'

She bit her lip.

'She's not had an easy life and she's all bottled up inside and can't show what she feels, so she gives the wrong impression. But underneath she has a heart of gold.'

My mother rose, thus preventing further confidences, and

went into the kitchen to butter the crumpets.

I got up slowly from the floor, wondering about what my mother had just said and trying not to dislike Sybil. But it wasn't easy.

'Are you bringing the crumpets?' Sybil called exasperatedly, glaring round the dining room door. 'I've poured the tea and we're all waiting.'

And she stomped off across the hall.

At that moment I couldn't imagine her having a heart at all, and certainly not a heart of gold.

As I followed my mother into the cosy drawing room my father and younger brother were putting away the chess board, the Christmas decorations were still up and multi-coloured lights winked from the large tree in the corner. The whole impression was one of warmth and security, the heavy curtains drawn against the early winter's night and the firelight once again dancing on the fluted china cups as Sybil handed them round. I felt loved and safe and grateful for my mother's assurance that we, her family, were her most important guests – the most important people in her life in fact – and that only the best was good enough for us.

Perhaps this memory helped to sustain me during the tragic years which were to follow when the family unit in my home, as in so many other homes, was broken up and scattered. Great-grandmother's precious tea-set was smashed to smithereens when a bomb landed not far from our house, demolishing a lot of our treasures with it: treasures which, because of my mother's wise philosophy, had been well used before they were blown to pieces.

For some reason that winter Sunday afternoon nearly fifty years ago stamped itself indelibly on my mind. I think it taught me the importance of values which were so soon to be destroyed as the terrible holocaust hit Europe and, perhaps most important of all, the incomparable value of a family, and of family life.

I am sure that my mother never thought, when she faced

her cousin Sybil across the tea trolley in an argument over their grandmother's china, that her reply would make such an impression on her growing daughter. That her chance remark would contribute towards giving me the assurance I so needed in those war-torn years, when everything we had been brought up to believe in as lasting and permanent was scattered and shattered, and later help to set the pattern and perhaps even lay the foundations of her grandchildren's family life.

Chapter 2

THOSE BYGONE DAYS

I had always had a 'second home' at Great-Aunt Jessica's, and during the war years often spent my school holidays there, where my grandmother happened to be living at the time. Aunt Jessica was the eldest of my grandmother's five sisters and her house had always been a focal point where all the family congregated; and it was here that I heard about the 'skeleton' in the family cupboard which helped me to see Sybil in a different light.

There was a different kind of 'generation gap' in those days. We loved and respected our parents, but they were not our 'friends', there was none of the easy intimacy which exists between parents and children today. Had there been more openness between the generations when I was a child, I would have known of the tragedy in Sybil's life and, even if not fully understanding, I might not have resented her so deeply. But 'family secrets' were not for young ears, and so I was left in the dark.

It was Geraldine, my mother's youngest cousin, who uncovered this skeleton when we were alone together at Great-Aunt Jessica's one evening.

Geraldine, the daughter of Grannie's youngest sister, was only seven years older than I, and although I rather resented her calling my parents by their Christian names, we were firm friends and had spent many pre-war holidays together.

She had joined the WRNS at the outbreak of war and,

being stationed in the nearby town, spent most of her off-duty time at Aunt Jessica's.

This particular evening, Grannie and Aunt Jessica had gone to Evensong and Great-Uncle Freddie, Aunt Jessica's husband, who never went to church, had in spite of his eighty-odd years left the previous afternoon for a weekend fire-watching duty, leaving Geraldine and me alone.

We had been for a walk and as we came back into the house Geraldine tossed her WRNS cap on to a chair. I picked it up and was standing in front of the hall mirror trying it on at various angles, when there was a sudden scuffle and chattering along the picture rail followed by a piercing shriek.

'Owe, you blighter,' Geraldine yelled, 'get DOWN!'

But the monkey had no intention of getting down.

He squatted where he had landed, on Geraldine's head, and calmly picked his nose.

Percy was Uncle Freddie's pet, one of the souvenirs he had brought back with him from West Africa, and was supposed to be confined to the 'jungle', an overcrowded, untidy room off the hall where Uncle Freddie kept tigers' heads, elephants' tusks, a stuffed baby crocodile and Egbert, a bald screeching white cockatoo. The jungle was supposedly where Uncle Freddie worked, but as he appeared never to have done a stroke of work in his life, it was the place where he was to be found drinking whisky and smoking a long pipe away from all the females in his household . . .

Percy usually sat on the arm of Uncle Freddie's old leather armchair, or on the brass fender at his master's feet, contentedly eating bananas, periodically engaging in a shrieking competition with Egbert. But occasionally, when he sensed Aunt Jessica's absence, he would scramble nimbly round the picture frame and drop on any unsuspecting person who happened to be underneath.

Geraldine now clawed wildly at the monkey, who bent down and smartly bit her finger.

'Quick,' Geraldine squealed, 'get the soda siphon, it's on

the desk in the jungle, and squirt it in his eyes. Without Uncle Freddie it's the only way to dislodge him.'

I rushed into the blacked-out jungle and grabbed the siphon.

Egbert rocked and screeched from his perch as I dashed past him and back into the hall, holding the bottle clutched to my chest like a machine gun and, with a deft spurt, sent a short sharp spray of soda water into the monkey's eyes.

'Owch,' yelled Geraldine, 'you've soaked me too.'

'Sorry,' I breathed, ducking as Percy, adding his screeches to those of Egbert, leapt angrily from Geraldine's auburn curls and aimed at mine.

Another deft squirt sent him leaping to the picture rail, but not before he had landed heavily on my head, pushed the WRNS hat over my eyes and sent me flying.

I fell in a heap on the stairs, clutching the soda siphon, the hat still in place but somewhat battered and lurching drunkenly over one ear.

Geraldine looked down at me and began to giggle.

'Anyone coming in now would take you for Aunt Prudence,' she laughed.

Aunt Prudence was Sybil's mother, the only one of Grannie's five sisters I had never met. In fact, her name was never mentioned in my presence and if ever I walked in on a conversation about her, it always stopped abruptly.

'What do you mean?' I gasped.

'You look just like her,' Geraldine laughed. 'She apparently dresses up in the oddest clothes and once walked into the Town Hall and demanded to see the mayor wearing Uncle Fergus' boots and his bowler hat.'

I sank down on a chair in the dimly lit hall and slowly removed the hat.

'Do you know her?' I whispered.

'I've never actually *met* her,' Geraldine answered, 'but I've heard the weirdest stories about her.'

Something I'd heard Grannie once say to Great-Aunt

Jessica came back to me; 'Fergus should have had Prudence put away years ago . . .'

And then I'd looked up from the jigsaw I was doing and the conversation had abruptly ceased.

Great-Uncle Fergus was Aunt Prudence's husband and I liked him enormously. He had grey curly hair with ginger streaks and a bushy ginger moustache and his bright blue eyes looked as if they were about to pop out of his head. His voice had a delightful Scottish burr and he always carried peppermints in the pocket of his old tweed jacket, which he distributed liberally to any of the children who happened to be around.

'What's the matter with Great-Aunt Prudence?' I enquired, trying to give the appearance of not really being interested in case Geraldine, like all the aunts, would immediately clamp down and consider me too young to know.

'She went funny when John was born.'

John was Sybil's younger brother.

'That's why Sybil and John have practically been brought up by Aunt Jessica.'

'But funny how?' I pursued.

'I don't know,' Geraldine answered reflectively. 'I've never met her, but Mumsy told me that she's ruined Sybil's life.'

Geraldine always referred to her mother as 'Mumsy'.

'Sybil was engaged once,' Geraldine continued confidentially, sitting down beside me. 'It was years ago, but when her fiancé heard about Aunt Prudence he broke it off. Apparently she chased him across the lawn brandishing Uncle Fergus' dress sword when he came to see him about marrying Sybil, and Andrew gave her up after that.'

'How awful,' I whispered, remembering my mother's words to me on that far-off Sunday afternoon, and beginning to see Sybil in a different light.

'I believe it was,' Geraldine said sadly. 'Sybil completely changed after that. She hasn't been home for years and her mother turned right against her.'

So that was why Uncle Fergus and Sybil always met at Aunt Jessica's. I had never understood the reason before, nor why whenever he came to visit us it was always on his own. But now the picture was gradually becoming clear in my mind.

'But what about John?' I enquired.

John was Sybil's elder brother.

'Oh *he* can go home,' Geraldine replied. 'It's only Sybil who drives Aunt Prudence berserk.'

I removed the dented hat and sat fingering it absently.

'Poor Sybil,' I murmured, as gradually the skeleton, the pain in Sybil's life, came to light. And remorse for my hard feelings towards her began to tug at me.

'But John's married,' I went on after a pause.

'Yes, he is,' Geraldine replied, 'but Aunt Prudence has never met his wife, she doesn't even know she's got a granddaughter. Jolly tough on Uncle Fergus, he only ever sees little Laura if they bring her to Aunt Jessica's.'

'But does Aunt Prudence live near here?' I enquired.

'Just down the road,' I heard Geraldine reply matter-of-factly.

'*I* didn't know?'

'Uncle Fergus brought her here when she went "funny". He thought that being near Aunt Jessica might help – there's seventeen years between them and Aunt Jessica's more like her mother than her sister; at least since Grandmother died she apparently always regarded Aunt Jessica as a mother image.'

Geraldine paused and seemed thoughtful.

'You'd have thought Mumsy would have done that,' she mused, 'she was only two when Grandmother died.'

I nodded absently, wondering vaguely why Geraldine's mother, not mine, hadn't inherited the disputed tea-set. It would have seemed more normal for her to have some tangible souvenir of the mother she had never known.

Geraldine stretched and yawned.

'Go on,' I insisted, terrified lest she would change the subject and I should not at last be able to piece together all the odd phrases I had gleaned about Great-Aunt Prudence over the years.

'Not much else to tell really,' Geraldine replied. 'Aunt Jessica could tell you more.'

'Don't think she would,' I answered gloomily.

'Perhaps not. All I know is that Uncle Fergus and Aunt Prudence live in that old house on the corner, the one with the high stone walls around it, and that she hardly ever goes out. All the sisters feel that Uncle Fergus should have put her in some kind of home years ago as she's ruined John and Sybil's lives, well certainly Sybil's. But he never would.'

Geraldine absently picked up the battered WRNS hat.

'Can't be much of a life for him,' she said, knocking it into shape.

I nodded, thinking how many times over the years I had passed the house on the corner without ever knowing who lived there behind those high walls and I shivered involuntarily, wondering whether my great-aunt might not have rushed out and attacked me with a sword had she known who I was.

'Is she very violent?' I enquired.

'Apparently not at all,' Geraldine replied, 'except with Sybil.'

'How awful for Sybil,' I murmured.

'It is,' Geraldine went on, 'but it's worse for Uncle Fergus, and he's such a poppet. Everyone wonders what will happen when he dies.'

Geraldine sighed.

'She might die first,' I volunteered.

'She might,' Geraldine mused, 'but it's hardly likely. Aunt Prudence apparently hasn't changed over the years, the strain's been all on Uncle Fergus, and he *is* fifteen years older than her.'

She paused and looked at me, her green eyes very bright.

'I *did* see her once,' she said confidentially.

'When?' I enquired.

'Oh, many years ago. Mumsy and I were staying here and we went for a walk in the park one afternoon. I remember I ran on ahead with my hoop and when I looked back Mumsy had stopped and was talking to a lady sitting on a bench. I thought it was funny, the lady looked straight ahead as if she didn't see or hear her, then Uncle Fergus arrived and he and Mumsy exchanged a few words and Mumsy walked away. The lady didn't even move, she just kept staring in front of her as if she didn't see anyone. When Mumsy came up to me she had tears streaming down her cheeks.'

Geraldine paused.

'I'd never seen her cry before,' she went on softly, and gave her hat a final bash. 'When I asked her what was the matter she just said "That was your Aunt Prudence". I felt so sorry for her, for both of them. Aunt Prudence doesn't even speak to Aunt Jessica when she goes to see her.'

'Poor Sybil,' I breathed again.

'Yes, it's awful, isn't it? I remember when she was engaged she and Andrew used to come and stay. I was only about five at the time and they used to play snap with me. Then one day I went into Mumsy's room and found Sybil crying in her arms and when I asked where Andrew was Mumsy shushed me and told me to go and play. That must have been when he broke it off.'

Geraldine sighed.

'Sybil's a completely different person now, she used to be such fun. But what a life she's had, one long tragedy and now she can only meet her father in secret.'

There was a sudden noisy eruption followed by the crash of the heavy front door as Uncle Freddie's huge bulk burst into the hall.

'Oh glory,' giggled Geraldine, 'here comes Whiskers.'

Whiskers was a nickname we younger ones had long ago given to Great-Uncle Freddie, who never kissed us as the other uncles did but stooped from his vast height and insisted on rubbing noses. It was apparently a custom he had learned when living in Africa with the pygmies, and he'd insisted on greeting his long-suffering family in this way ever since.

Uncle Freddie was true to form this evening, rushing into the dimly lit hall, the only Englishman of that era to be seen wearing a cone-shaped black fur hat with dangling earflaps, a relic of his Arctic travels, crushed underneath his ARP helmet.

'Ho, ho, ho,' he chortled, seeing us sitting there, me still clutching the soda bottle in my arms. 'You two girls been at my whisky, have you?'

He looked like a cross between Father Christmas and the late Tsar of Russia, with his short bristly white beard, bushy white eyebrows and tousled white hair peeping out from beneath his steel helmet.

He and Aunt Jessica had never had any children, so all the nieces and nephews down to the second generation had been adopted by them, and spent school holidays racing all over their house and garden, discovering the treasures stored in every room.

Looking back, it was not surprising that they had remained childless, for Uncle Freddie had spent the greater part of his married life roaming round the world, living with pygmies and Eskimos and Aborigines and remote tribes on undiscovered desert islands, leaving his wife at home to cope with her five sisters and their children. He was a law unto himself and had never gone to church with the rest of us, having marinated a religion of his own from the various tribes and cultures with which he had lived.

He fascinated we children, especially when he told us tales of Zulus and fuzzy-wuzzies, as he called them, and demonstrated how to use the lethal spears, now hanging at the top of the stairs, which he had brought back from his travels.

Uncle Freddie was a true eccentric, and in spite of his hazy idea of God, was, in all other aspects, intensely Victorian English with a strong mistrust of 'foreigners' which, in his estimation, was anyone living south of Folkestone. He even went so far on occasions as to consider Scotland as enemy territory and, although he was great friends with Uncle Fergus and always delighted to see him, had been heard to mutter that all Prudence's problems had sprung from marrying a foreigner.

His travels had broadened him in some ways, but certainly not in others, and his unpredictable behaviour had, on occasion, caused Aunt Jessica, who was the most conservative of old ladies, acute embarrassment. He became especially dotty when a dear French friend whom Aunt Jessica had known since her teens was around. Madame de Rougemont always came to tea when she was in England and had once been startled out of her wits by Uncle Freddie bursting into the drawing room wearing baggy khaki shorts and a topee, brandishing one of the spears plucked from the head of the stairs for the occasion.

Glaring down at his wife's terrified guest from under his bushy eyebrows he had bellowed, 'Are the French out of Fashoda yet?'

'Freddie dear,' Aunt Jessica had apparently pleaded, putting down her tea cup, 'do please come in more quietly. You've quite startled poor Amélie.'

Whereupon Uncle Freddie had retreated, glowering, muttering 'Waterloo' menacingly between his teeth.

On another occasion he had belligerently brought up the Siege of Mafeking, for which poor Amélie de Rougemont's countrymen could in no way be held responsible.

Mercifully, as far as we know, he had never inflicted a nose-rubbing session on her, which would certainly have terrified Madame de Rougemont even more than his explosive intrusion on the tea party had done.

But Great-Uncle Freddie was a delight to us younger ones, none of whom was in the least intimidated, but rather hugely amused, by his growlings, which I think pleased him. I had been sent to stay with them for as long as I could remember and loved the spooky old house, even though I spent many a night suffocating under the blankets, terrified of even putting my head above the covers because of the stuffed white polar bear, with its staring glassy eyes and jagged teeth, which was standing on its hind legs in a corner of the room opposite my bed.

I don't think that anyone nowadays would expect a highly imaginative little girl to share a bedroom with a polar bear, but perhaps that explains the particular pre-war brand of generation gap.

Maybe they did not understand or even consider a child's sensibilities in quite the way we do now. Or perhaps my great-aunt and uncle understood me only too well and had decided that it was better for me to face up to my fears in the security and comfort of the family home, rather than come face to face with them in a more brutal fashion when I found myself out alone in the world.

Certainly Aunt Jessica paid no attention to my fears or my pleas for company when going to the bathroom after dark, or even for permission to leave the door open.

The only reply I ever received was: 'Certainly not, whatever next.'

It may sound an odd request but behind the bathroom door hung a large oil painting of one of Uncle Freddie's ancestors wearing a frilly ruff and a pointed black beard and, in the dim gas light, he seemed to leer menacingly down at me. I had tried closing my eyes but was always compelled to open them, masochistically fascinated by the horror his unsmiling face produced. Looking back, I can't understand why such a treasure should have been hung in the bathroom in the first place, but then neither did I understand why Uncle Freddie's stuffed polar bear should live in the bedroom.

Aunt Jessica's voice broke in on the ho-hoing and nose rubbing.

'Geraldine,' she called, 'what time do you have to go, dear?'
So she and my grandmother were back from Evensong.

I knew there would be no more gossiping for Geraldine and
me that evening.

'Must catch the nine-eighteen train, Aunt Jessica,'
Geraldine called back. 'It just gets me back in time for our ten
o'clock curfew.'

'Very well dear,' Aunt Jessica had answered, 'we'd better
have supper straight away and then your uncle will walk
down to the station with you.'

'Oh no,' Geraldine groaned, 'that means more nose
rubbings on the platform. And I expect he'll wear that
DREADFUL hat as well!'

I giggled and Geraldine sighed resignedly as we sauntered
towards the dining room.

'And *all* the girls from my billet are bound to be on the
train,' she wailed, casting her emerald eyes dramatically up to
the ceiling in mock despair.

There were to be no more confidences between Geraldine
and me because she was posted away soon afterwards. I
didn't see her again until just after the war, when we all met at
Aunt Jessica's to wish her goodbye before she and her
bridegroom left for Kenya.

But it was a strangely quiet house in which we all gathered.

Great-Uncle Freddie had died a month before peace was
declared, a massive stroke taking his life in one swift blow. It
was a blessing, really, as none of us could have envisaged that
vast, laughing frame wasting away as an invalid. After his
master's death Percy just pined away and died too, and an
abnormally subdued Egbert took up residence in the
conservatory.

Robin, Geraldine's older brother, had survived Dunkirk
only to be killed, not fighting gloriously with his regiment,
but during an air raid on London whilst on embarkation
leave. When Geraldine left England her widowed mother, my
Great-Aunt Gwendolen sold her home and went to live with

her two older sisters. They made a formidable trio, but posed a conundrum for the younger generation who had always nicknamed Grannie and Aunt Jessica 'Arsenic and Old Lace', and now were at a loss for a suitable epithet to encompass the three of them.

I never did meet Great-Aunt Prudence, but after my conversation with Geraldine on that wartime Sunday evening, as my mother had told me I would, I gradually discovered the real Sybil, and came to love the ill-tempered cousin whose visits I had so dreaded in my youth.

She even became a welcome visitor to my own home after I married, and my children neither disliked, resented nor were afraid of her. Just as we, the previous generation, had been completely unawed by Uncle Freddie's growlings, so my children were able to take Sybil as she was and see through her to the soft centre beneath.

But in the intervening years, like me, Sybil had changed. And, like me, the change had come when she met Jesus as her personal Saviour and was able to hand over to him the aching void and the loneliness in her life and receive his peace in return.

When I became a committed, born again Christian, remembering Sybil, I understood Jesus's words when he told us not to judge by outward appearances. He cited the Pharisees as examples of whitewashed sepulchres, clean and shining on the outside but rotten on the inside. Sybil was just the opposite, and how grateful I was to my mother for sowing those seeds that Sunday afternoon so long ago, telling me that Sybil was not what she appeared to be.

But sometimes it is beyond our human power to dig through to that centre, the hurt goes too deep. Then only the spirit of Jesus flowing through us can bring about the miracle of transformation, of a changed life. For, as with Sybil, only his love is able to penetrate the masks and reveal the ulcers and the bleeding heart beneath and, having revealed it, pour his healing balm into the open wound.

As a family, before the war, we had all been regular, faithful churchgoers. But we didn't talk about Jesus because none of us knew him personally, none of us had or, I suspect, even knew it was possible to have, a day by day walk with the living Lord. We said God or Christ at church services or in our bedside prayers at night, but Jesus was not a word which was pronounced easily in conventional Anglican circles fifty years ago. It smelt of fanaticism and didn't fit in with good manners.

Sybil's earthly family would have done anything to help and comfort her, but they were powerless because their human love was not able to reach down and heal the aching heart she hid. So often our ability to love and to receive love relates closely to our experience of being loved, and Sybil had twice known rejection in her life, first from her mother and then from her fiancé. And, because she was afraid of further pain, she warded off any attempt by her extended family to love her.

It was only, shortly after the end of the war, when she met Jesus the great healer who never rejects us, whose love is divine and everlasting and discovered that she was one of God's children made in his image, that she was healed and found peace. She accepted Jesus's love, which he offers each one of us, and claimed her rightful heritage, membership of God's family and his gift of eternal life – and that made all the difference. She not only became a new creature in him, but a new person, a changed person, even a lovable person to all of us.

Chapter 3

THE SECRET

Jesus was born into a family.

He could have come into the world in any number of ways, but God chose to have him born into a very humble Jewish family: his father was a carpenter and his mother 'just a housewife'. He came into this close-knit unit in which I and many of my generation grew up and which, in spite of quarrels, internal dissension and differing personalities, nevertheless remained intact and gave the next generation a sense of security which, sadly, many of today's children, with the scattered family unit and the one-parent family, no longer know.

My grandmother was a very important part of my young life.

She always wore a black velvet ribbon, with a circle of tiny pearls in the middle, round her throat and a very beautiful old cameo brooch, as well as a gold fob watch which my grandfather, whom she always referred to as 'my dear Rob', had given her when they became engaged back in 1892.

As her only granddaughter, I inherited these souvenirs when she died. They were later all stolen, and never recovered, which taught me one of Jesus's lessons, 'not to store up treasures here on earth where thieves and rust can destroy them'. I also saw her diamond engagement ring, which I had forgotten to remove before washing Bee's hair one evening, disappear down the plug hole. THAT was never recovered either, at least not by me, in spite of all our attempts. So, as she had sold her home and contents after my grandfather's death, I have very few tangible souvenirs of her: but I do remember her, and especially her vivid, chameleon-like personality.

We grandchildren were members of her 'secret club', in which we all had our appointed places. I was her 'friend', my brother Geoffrey her 'chum' and our cousin Tom who, being an only child and just a few months older than Geoffrey, often came to stay, was her 'pal'. An unusual word for Grannie to use, but perhaps we had chosen our names ourselves, I can't remember. I don't think her third grandson, Brian, ever had a special name. He was her only son's child and arrived towards the end of the war when we three were in our teens and the family unit was already becoming slightly threadbare.

Although we had this special relationship with her I do not mean to imply that she was by any means the story book image of a grandmother: warm, plump, placid and rosy-cheeked, cosily sitting knitting by an open fire with the kettle singing merrily on the hob.

No, my grandmother was exactly the opposite.

She was beautiful, elegant, self-centred and very quarrel-some with all the members of her family. But to outsiders and to her grandchildren she was a delight, full of charm and endless amusing and exciting stories.

When she came to stay with us it was always a difficult time for my mother because Grannie criticised everything and quarrelled endlessly with her elder daughter. This pattern was repeated throughout her family, as she also quarrelled with her son. My Aunt Dodo, who was her middle child, never quarrelled with anyone – which probably explains why she was spared grandmother's visits. For although she frequently descended on us, and on her son and his wife, she rarely went to stay with Aunt Dodo and her husband.

The strange thing about grandmother was that she seemed

to prefer her in-laws to her children and got on famously with her sons-in-law and my uncle's wife. She also was held in adoration by her grandchildren; but then fifty years ago children didn't argue with their parents, let alone their grandparents.

Grannie had her own way of life which she imposed on everyone with whom she went to stay. Having been left a widow at fifty-seven, she gave up her home and went to live in hotels, which suited her admirably. She was a great letter writer and conversationalist, and people who met her could never understand why her children were not all longing to have her stay with them permanently – she was such a charming old lady. And indeed she was when she wanted to be.

In a way, she was not unlike Sybil, except that Sybil was tart with everyone and her mask hid a deep hurt, whereas I don't think Grannie even wore a mask. She was just like that. Spoilt by her father, spoilt by an adoring husband, she found it hard not to continue to be spoilt for the rest of her life by her children. I suppose it must have been difficult to be expected to break with a pattern of life which had continued for over half a century.

Grannie never got up before midday, but we often crept in with her breakfast tray and curled up on her bed whilst she told us stories of her youth and her travels.

Her mother had died when she was ten years old. Great-Aunt Jessica, who was nine years older, and Great-Aunt Julia, who came immediately after her, were perhaps more able to cope with such a traumatic experience than Grannie was. But it's strange the way family patterns seem to repeat themselves. My great-grandmother had an older married sister, childless like Aunt Jessica, who, as Aunt Jessica had later done with her younger sister Prudence's children, had taken Grannie and her brother and sisters into her home and brought them up whilst my great-grandfather went travelling after his wife died. He apparently went round the world three times, twice in a sailing vessel and once by steam. No mean feat in the middle of the nineteenth century.

Grannie was her father's favourite, perhaps because of the seven year gap between herself and Julia which, in those days, must surely have meant the disappointment of miscarriages and still-births. She was the only one of his children to whom great-grandfather gave a nickname: he called her 'Toddy', no one ever knew why, and Great-Uncle Cecil, Grannie's only brother, continued the custom right up to the time of his death. None of her sisters ever called her by anything but her proper name.

I think my great-grandfather must have been almost as eccentric as Uncle Freddie for, when he gave up racing round the globe, he apparently went to live off the north-east coast of England in an old, obviously abandoned lighthouse (which he presumably bought) and spent his days peering out to sea through a long telescope or cycling madly across wet sand and round the local town on an old penny-farthing bicycle. No doubt to the delight and also the consternation of the local inhabitants, who probably did not expect such odd behaviour in an elderly gentleman.

My mother told me of the times she had visited him and the fun she and her cousin Elliot, one of Aunt Julia's six sons who was exactly her age, had had racing up and down the narrow winding lighthouse stairs – a terribly dangerous thing to do, especially when hampered by the long petticoats she obviously wore at the end of the last century, which detail did not seem to have bothered my great-grandfather in the slightest. My mother confided in me that she didn't go often, possibly because her parents realised the danger, but stayed instead with her paternal grandparents, who weren't nearly so much fun.

In the 1880s my great-grandfather took my grandmother all over Europe and on our morning visits to her bedroom she often described to us the South of France as it then was: a beautiful unspoiled coastline slowly becoming fashionable because of Queen Victoria's frequently spending the bleak winter months after Christmas enjoying the Mediterranean sunshine. We used to beg her to repeat these stories again and again endlessly, especially the one about how her foot got stuck between the boat and the quay at Rotterdam. She also told us how in southern Italy, even in those days, it had been difficult for a young girl to escape the admiring glances of the local men strolling in the streets. She had even been to Russia and I remember asking if her sisters and Great-Uncle Cecil had not felt jealous of her being so obviously their father's favourite. But Grannie had merely looked at me in her regal way and I had felt crushed. She seemed to take it as her right that she should be the privileged one, and it appears that the others accepted it that way too.

Grannie's one redeeming feature was her great love for her younger brother. He seemed to matter to her more than anyone, perhaps even more than her husband had done. Unfortunately I never met my grandfather, who died before my first birthday. We were living in Malta at the time, where I was born, and as it was then a ten day voyage by sea to England I had not been taken back and introduced to my grandparents.

Looking back, I find this same pattern running right through the fabric of my family. Grannie and Great-Uncle Cecil had apparently been inseparable. My mother and her younger brother had also had this tight bond between them, completely bypassing my Aunt Dodo, the middle one of my grandmother's children. And my brother and I have always been very close. As I look at my own family unit I see that there is a strong bond which, even though they are now grown up, still exists between Bee and Yves, who is seven years her junior. And I can't help wondering how Bee's little daughter will feel towards her baby brother and whether, as they grow older, this affinity will continue to weave its way into the family pattern through the future generations.

God knew what he was doing when he created the family.

That unit where members can quarrel and disagree and ignore each other, but where love all the same goes deep, and when trouble hits one of its members, as I have found, the hidden bond is there and can be counted on to withstand the strain.

And I think Grannie knew this too.

She was very intelligent and although all her life she ran roughshod over her family I think in her own way she loved them. She certainly knew that she could show them her 'other' face, her tantrums, whereas to people she met in hotels she could only show the charming side of her character.

But with her young brother she was different.

I often went with her to visit him and she seemed almost protective. Great-Uncle Cecil had never done very much with his life and in old age seemed quite content to continue to drift. Perhaps the overwhelming burden of six sisters and a father who was never there had affected his character and crushed him; I don't know, but Grannie always treated him as her little brother and was fiercely protective of this weak, apparent failure. And they shared a dreadful secret, another family skeleton, a burden which should never have been theirs and for which they so obviously were not responsible.

'It was just after mother died,' Grannie began on one of those mornings when we were curled up on her bed begging for stories. 'Father had gone abroad and we were left with Aunt and Uncle as usual. It was Easter time and they had taken a house by the sea, thinking that the change of air would do us all good.'

She never referred to her mother's sister and her husband as anything other than 'Aunt and Uncle'; they didn't appear to have any names, and I don't think Grannie liked them very much. Perhaps she had the same relationship with them as a girl as she had with the rest of the family when she grew up.

'Cecil and I were sent for our morning walk along the beach with Julia and told to take Daisy with us. Julia went on ahead because she wanted to pick up shells for her collection and she told Cecil and me to look after Daisy.'

Grannie stopped. I don't know whether it was for effect, she'd have made a wonderful actress, or whether even after all those years she still felt emotion.

'Go on,' we whispered, awed by whatever terrible secret might soon be coming to light.

'Well, we didn't,' she said simply.

'What happened?' we asked.

'We lost her,' Grannie stated flatly. 'Cecil and I took off our boots and stockings and paddled. It was strictly forbidden, and the water was icy, then we chased each other along the sand to get our feet dry so that Aunt would never know what we'd done. When we looked back, we couldn't see Daisy.'

She paused, and we didn't dare say anything in case she opted not to continue. Grannie was a creature of whims and could very well have decided that that was enough for one morning, so we held our breath and waited.

After a few seconds I felt I would burst if I didn't hear the end of the story.

'Did you find her?' I whispered.

'Yes, we found her,' Grannie went on quietly. 'She was sitting beside an upturned boat not far from where we'd left her.'

'So it was all right then?' I breathed.

'No, it was far from all right,' Grannie went on. 'There was some rubbish nearby and Daisy had found a dirty carrot and was eating it.'

I felt let down: *that* didn't seem very terrible to me.

Grannie's sense of drama realised that her audience was disappointed, but she had left the best to the last.

'We brushed her down and went back to the house, threatening her with all sorts of terrible punishments if she told Aunt what had happened. She was only six and she started crying, so we threatened her with worse things if she didn't stop.'

We laughed then. We'd all been through that.

'But that wasn't the end,' Grannie said softly. 'That night Daisy woke up screaming in agony. She had terrible stomach pains.' Grannie knew how to produce dramatic effect and had captured our interest again.

'The doctor was sent for and he stayed the rest of the night.' She paused and sighed deeply.

'I'll never forget that morning. Cecil and I crouched outside Daisy's room filled with remorse, we knew that the pain was caused by the carrot but we didn't dare to say anything. Just before lunch Aunt and the doctor came out of the room and Aunt was crying. I'd never seen her cry before, not even at mother's funeral, but she was crying then. The doctor told us to go back to the nursery and he took Aunt by the arm and they went downstairs and closed the dining room door. Later Uncle came upstairs and told us that Daisy had died.'

I remember that I began to cry. It seemed too awful.

'Cecil and I never told anyone about the carrot,' Grannie said quietly. 'But we knew that that was what had caused her death. We'd killed our little sister.'

She paused again as the three of us sniffed and sobbed.

'Daisy had died because we'd run away and forgotten about her when Aunt had told us to look after her.'

'Oh Grannie,' I remember saying, tears streaming down my face. 'Perhaps it wasn't the carrot, perhaps it was something else. Maybe Daisy had some dreadful disease.'

'She was all right until that morning,' Grannie said simply.

'Did you ever tell Aunt?' I asked.

'Never,' Grannie replied. 'We didn't dare. Daisy was very special to her because she had been named after her (so Aunt did have a name after all – though we never discovered whether Uncle did). I don't think she'd ever have forgiven us if she'd known.'

I think I realised then, young as I was, that Grannie had never been able to forgive herself.

'Did Aunt Jessica know?' I asked.

I couldn't imagine anything happening in the family

without Aunt Jessica knowing.

'She does now,' Grannie answered. 'But it wasn't until after your mother was born that I was able to tell her, and even then Cecil wasn't happy about her knowing.'

She sighed deeply.

'But it had all happened so long ago.'

'And did she blame you?' I pursued.

'I don't think so,' Grannie replied. 'But I blamed myself.'

There was a silence and then suddenly Grannie's pensive mood changed.

'It's time you children went downstairs,' she suddenly said. 'Off you go.'

And scrambling off the bed we went, I think thankfully. We had had enough emotion for one morning.

Looking back, of course, it was so obvious that Grannie and Great-Uncle Cecil were in no way responsible for Daisy's death. It could have been one of many critical illnesses but was most probably a sudden, acute appendicitis which, in the late 1870s, was fatal. If only they had been able to confess their terrible secret, bring their guilt into the open, they need not have carried a burden which was far too heavy for their young shoulders, and carried it for the rest of their lives.

Chapter 4

FEAR AND GUILT

As a Christian, I realise just what a gift confession is.

How many terrible burdens do we try to carry alone simply because we do not know about the cleansing love and forgiveness of our Lord? The words 'he died on the cross for our sins, to free us from the burden of sin and guilt' have been so bandied about that sometimes they seem to have lost their true meaning.

We don't realise the enormity of the sacrifice which Jesus made when he came into the world as a helpless baby and, as a young man, hung for three terrible hours on a rough wooden cross, in total darkness of spirit and desolation, cut off from his Father who had sent him. And why? For he had done no wrong. Simply because he had promised to bear the sins of the whole world and, in so dying, obtain our forgiveness.

How many people are lying in hospital beds today not because of some physical pain but because of the dreadful pain of guilt, often far worse and more difficult to cure than physical agony.

Perhaps, as in my grandmother's and great-uncle's case, guilt for which they were not responsible, imaginary guilt which, if only confessed, can be seen for what it is: but guilt which, imaginary or real, so often darkens the life of the person who is crushed beneath its load.

And I do not say this lightly, for I have lain in such a

hospital bed myself; I have trodden the dreadful path of guilt.

I wonder if this tragedy, which happened when she was a little girl of just eleven and her brother only nine, may not have coloured the rest of my grandmother's life, of both their lives. It may explain why she was different from her sisters, more difficult to live with, argumentative, demanding, at times downright cruel to those she loved. For when we are hurt we so often want to lunge out and hit back, usually at those we love.

It may also explain why Great-Uncle Cecil did so little with his life. That early 'failure' may have given him the feeling that he was a failure in everything else, unable to be trusted, unable to carry out any task assigned to him.

If only they had been able to confess, to say what had happened that spring morning, to take the punishment which, in those strict Victorian days, would certainly have been meted out to them – not for 'killing' their little sister but for their disobedience in failing to look after her – they would have been relieved of that great burden. They would have been assured that an unwashed carrot had in no way caused Daisy's death; that even had she not eaten it the sudden illness which had so dramatically killed her would have attacked her anyway.

But such was the communication gap between adults and children in my grandmother's youth that, although the doctor certainly gave the reason for Daisy's sudden death, it was obviously not considered necessary to pass this information on to the younger children. And, as a consequence, fear and guilt caused Grannie and Great-Uncle Cecil to hold their tongues and carry the secret burden for the rest of their lives.

I think today's generation gap which everyone talks so much about would not have prevented modern children from confessing that act of disobedience which, on reflection, was not so terrible. For, in spite of what people say, there is far more communication between parents and children nowadays than there was even in my youth, and certainly more than existed during the last century. And, therefore, in many ways, less hurt because fears and guilt are able to be brought to the surface and not crushed into the depths of the subconscious... providing that there are parents who have the time to listen!

But even so, how many of us are hiding terrible secrets under our masks, beneath the faces we present to the outside world?

I know I hid many until the day when, after months of darkness, Jesus came into my life, until he broke through that black cloud of guilt and despair which had completely engulfed me and showed me that I could hide nothing from him. That although the 'world' saw only my 'outside', the 'outside' I chose to show them, he could see through the mask to the deep dark hidden recesses of my heart, to my innermost being. And, seeing the guilt, the pain and, yes, the sin, he still loved me and longed to cleanse and forgive me and make me whole again.*

If only my grandmother had known that truth.

If only someone in the church which she attended twice every Sunday throughout her life had been able to point out to her that passage in the New Testament which she repeated at every communion service, perhaps without fully understanding its meaning: 'If we claim to be without sin we deceive ourselves and the truth is not in us. If we confess our sins he is faithful and will forgive us our sins and purify us from all unrighteousness', (1 John 1:8,9) which proves that Jesus came into the world to save *sinners*, not *saints*! How different her life, and the lives of those around her, might have been.

For, in looking back, in spite of her selfishness, her domination of other people, her knack of always getting her own way in every situation, my grandmother was not, basically, a happy woman. And, being very like her, or so I'm

*The story of my conversion is told in *Eye of the Storm*.

told, I know that those attributes which I inherited from her do not bring true happiness.

They may bring temporary euphoria and satisfaction but, like a drug, once the effect has worn off, they leave only a sense of emptiness and a God-sized hole in the heart which only Jesus can fill. And I now know that until we meet him and recognise this truth so many of us carry this emptiness and dissatisfaction around with us behind a smiling face: it is an everlasting thirst which is never quenched. For only Jesus can satisfy our longings, supply our every need.

The sad thing is that, as we read in Revelation, he is standing at the door and knocking, waiting for us to open the door of our hearts and let him in. But so often we are deafened by the clamour and the glamour of the world and we don't hear him. Sadly, some of us never hear him, and go through life carrying our burdens, forever desperately seeking that 'something more' which is there all the time.

As I write this I think how terrible it must have been to lose a child in such circumstances, so brutally, because medical knowledge was not as far advanced as it is today. And how many families in the nineteenth century endured this agony, perhaps more than once?

But as I look around me I realise that even with the advanced medical technology of the late twentieth century people are even now losing their children, not by death, but just because the circumstances of life, and especially family life, are such that there is no longer any structure, and all the barriers are down. Life has become a kind of free-for-all without any set of rules or guidelines, and parents today lose their children sometimes far more tragically than through death. Many lose them through divorce or drugs or to the many religious sects, the false prophets as the Bible calls them, which are insidiously creeping into our western society.

These twentieth century false prophets often appear to young people, who are drifting or idealists, seeking a 'perfect society' or a meaning to life, to have the answer. In many cases they offer them love and security – usually a strange kind of love, certainly not the unconditional, selfless Calvary love which Jesus offers – and a set of rules and guidelines: all the things which were once the prerogative of the family unit and which, in spite of the many tomes written to the contrary telling us that children should be free to grow like weeds, is what children really need and want. That firm structure based on love and trust against which they can kick and test their strength when the time comes. And the sects seem to have understood this yearning and have cashed in on it, while many parents appear to have lost that vision and seem almost afraid to thwart their children in any way. Afraid in fact, to say no.

Are we afraid of losing their love?

Perhaps.

But a child who is truly loved is, as the Bible tells us, disciplined. It is so much easier to let them do as they like than to say no. And very often it is the young person who has been allowed this free rein who is attracted by the security which the discipline and structured life of the sects offers.

I sometimes wonder whether it would not be worse to lose a child to a sect than through death.

The Victorians had a structure to their lives, they went to church, and yet sometimes I think that their brand of Christianity was like the tail wagging the dog. God had become a habit and legalism had crept up on them, giving churchgoers a frontal lobotomy which left them alive but not living – not, that is, in the spiritual sense.

My grandmother and many of her generation didn't have this personal relationship with Jesus Christ which makes all the difference to life. For knowing him is the difference between night and day, between walking in a tunnel and suddenly bursting out of it into the light.

Chapter 5

ETERNITY

Some years ago my little boy explained eternity to me far better than I could ever have put it.

The subject had come up in one of our bedtime sessions and, not surprisingly, I had found it difficult to explain to a ten year old and a seven year old just what it meant. But, a few days later as we were driving along the road towards the neighbouring town, we plunged into the semi-darkness of an underpass, before coming out on the other side onto a long wide stretch of sunlit road. As we did so from the back seat our ten year old suddenly exclaimed:

'That's it Mummie, *now* I understand!'

'What do you understand?' I replied automatically.

'About eternity,' Yves said simply.

And to him, it was simple.

The assorted noises and rumbles from the back seat ceased. Eternity was a big, and slightly unusual, word for that age group.

'Remember, you were trying to explain to us about eternity the other night,' Yves went on.

I nodded.

'And we just couldn't understand, could we, how God's love could be everywhere, all over the world and he could see backwards and forwards and now, at the same time?'

I smiled, well remembering my struggles.

'Well, it's like the tunnel,' Yves triumphed. 'We can see

behind us and we can see in front and when we are going through it in the car, although it's all black for a minute, the sunshine and the light are still there all around us, only because of the walls we can't see them. But we know that at the other end of the tunnel there's an opening and when we go out through that it's light.'

He paused. There was something of his great-grandmother in Yves and he was enjoying the rapt attention of those sharing the back seat with him.

'Then suddenly,' he went on, 'pop, we're out of the tunnel into that bit of light and then *everything's* light and we can see all around us. There are no dark sides any more to stop us, just bigness and brightness. We can see in front and behind and all round at the same time, just like God can.'

I glanced up into the driving mirror. Yves was leaning forward with the others hanging on to his words. But the triumphant light was no longer in his china-blue eyes, instead they had a luminosity, an unusual brightness which was strangely soft and limpid, almost as if he were seeing a vision and was no longer with us.

'Life is like a dark tunnel,' he said softly, 'and when we die and go to heaven we come out of the tunnel and into God's sunshine.'

He paused and the silence was electric.

'And that's where Jesus will be waiting,' he ended simply.

For once there was silence in the car. The others were suddenly subdued, almost as if they realised that they had just heard something which was so simple and obvious, and yet strangely deep and prophetic; something they wouldn't find in books but which had been revealed to them through this highly strung, sensitive young boy who, at that moment, was truly seeing something which we didn't see.

It was a particularly lovely day, warm and mellow, and the effect of coming out of the semi-darkness into the shimmering afternoon was breathtaking.

For a moment tears of joy and gratitude filled my eyes as I

glanced up into the driving mirror and saw my son's pensive gaze reflected back at me.

'Jesus,' I murmured, 'how can I thank you. I've read so many high-powered tomes trying to understand and explain eternity and infinity, and yet it took my child's simple faith to take me off my pedestal and show me the truth.'

And I wondered there and then at this mystery of life and death which is so crystal clear and yet which we make so complicated. But then didn't Jesus say that there are truths which will be hidden from the wise and learned and revealed to little children. Sometimes we truly are blinded and cannot see the wood for the trees, the obvious which is staring us in the face.

So many Bible truths are simple and yet we try to complicate them. I understood that summer afternoon just what the Psalmist meant when he said: 'From the lips of children and infants you have ordained praise,' and also Jesus's words that unless we become as little children we cannot understand the things of God or indeed enter the kingdom of heaven.

Faith doesn't require intellect or learning; it merely needs a heart open and ready to receive the love of Jesus. Even a heart which is coarsened and stained by sin can be washed clean and purified, as we read in Isaiah 'though your sins are like scarlet they shall be as white as snow.'

Not very long afterwards, Yves' words and their implication, came back to me with tremendous force when we heard of a man, blackened by sin who had, through hearing those words of Isaiah, literally burst out of the tunnel, into the light.

Chapter 6

WHY SHOULD I FEAR?

My husband Jacques had to go to Florida on business and he invited the two youngest boys and me to accompany him, casually mentioning that as the plane stopped at Nassau en route we could spend a few days in the Bahamas on the way.

We didn't need to be asked twice!

As our plane circled over Nassau airport and prepared to land the boys and I looked eagerly through the window at the scene below. Although it was by now 2 a.m. European time and we had been up since six the morning before, excitement had kept us buoyant and full of expectation. And our first glimpse of the Bahamas did not disappoint us.

We drove from the airport through the warm, velvety black evening, the tall gently waving palm trees, the soft lap of the translucent sea against the white sandy beaches and the round yellow Caribbean moon were just as the tourist brochures had promised us the Bahamas would be.

The sun-drenched days passed in a dream.

I had the feeling I was living on some fabulous pre-war Hollywood South Sea Island film set as we wandered through the picturesque waterfront market, wearing large straw hats, plunged into the frothing surf, leaned on the harbour wall gazing dreamily at the millionaires' yachts and dug our teeth into whole iced pineapples wobbling on a stick like golden candy floss.

When one of Jacques' colleagues invited us to lunch on a

luxurious tourist boat anchored off Paradise Island, and we sat gazing out over the incredibly blue ocean eating exotic food to the gentle throb of a calypso band, I no longer believed that we were still on this time-ridden planet. Afterwards he drove us through the lovely residential areas of Nassau, sleepy under the shimmering haze of the afternoon sun, then wove his way through the colourful crowds thronging the steep main streets, pointing out the former British Governor's Palace and the 'Queen's Prison' as it was still called.

That name rang a bell for me, and as the car turned towards the coast road, I told our friend an extraordinary story I had heard about a murderer who had been befriended by a prison visitor during his time in the death cell there.

Henry drew up in front of a very English looking cricket pitch on the edge of the shore and, turning to me said quietly: 'I was that prison visitor.'

For a moment I sat, stunned, but as we walked over to sit in the shade of the trees this courteous, middle-aged man told us the story.

'He was only in his thirties,' Henry said softly, 'but a hardened criminal, a real tough nut who had spent long terms in prison for armed robbery, violence and finally been condemned to death for a particularly brutal murder. But, after the sentence was pronounced, he completely changed.'

Henry paused as a tray was placed on the table in front of us.

'He'd never shown any mercy for his victims,' he went on, pouring each one of us a glass of fruit juice, 'yet at heart he was a coward, terrified of death and he became physically ill. He couldn't eat or sleep, he vomited incessantly . . . and yet he didn't even inspire pity, he was so venomous and bitter.'

Only the sharp click of a cricket ball hitting against the bat broke the silence as Henry drew thirstily on the thick syrupy liquid which was crushed from passion fruit.

'I asked to see him on one of my regular visits to the prison but was advised against it because of his violence. Yet something prompted me to insist and finally I was let into his cell.'

'Weren't you frightened?' gasped Christopher, our youngest, his eyes like saucers.

Henry smiled across at him. 'Apprehensive, yes,' he answered, 'frightened, no.'

'What happened?' I prompted.

'He just stared at me with hatred in his eyes,' Henry answered sadly, 'then he spat and turned away. I sat down and tried to talk to him but he cursed and abused me: he shouted and screamed and rattled the bars of his cell to drown my voice and finally threw himself on his bunk, covering his head with his pillow.'

Henry sighed. 'So I left. But a few days later I went back ... it was the same scene all over again.'

He leaned forward and placed his empty glass on the table before continuing.

'I suppose a younger man would have taken the prison authorities' advice and given up, but I felt a deep sympathy for this man who had been rejected all his life and was now trying to force me to reject him. And I saw through to the frightened boy beneath.'

Henry removed his glasses and wiped them thoughtfully.

'Then one day the mask began to crack and instead of hurling abuse at me he just sat on his bunk staring at the floor. I started to tell him about the love of Jesus and how no sin is so vile that it cannot be forgiven if the sinner will repent. He didn't react: he didn't even raise his head when the warder told me it was time to leave! But I was encouraged, and I went back.'

Both boys were now leaning forward, hanging on his every word.

'He didn't greet me when I arrived or say goodbye to me when I left. Yet one day I read from Isaiah "though your sins be scarlet they shall be as white as snow" and when I looked up there were tears streaming down his face. I went over and sat down beside him putting my arm round his shoulders; he didn't resist and his whole body began to shake with sobs.'

Tears were now beginning to sting at the back of my eyelids.

'For a few moments neither of us spoke,' Henry continued, 'but those tears, the first he had shed since his mother abandoned him when he was eight years old, began his healing, washing the hatred and bitterness out of his heart. And, when they were spent, I knelt beside his bunk and offered a prayer of thanks.'

Henry removed his Panama hat and wiped his brow.

'To my utter amazement he quietly replied "Amen",' he said, replacing the hat on his head. 'It was less than a week before the date set for his execution and I asked permission to visit him each afternoon. His defences were down and I was able to sit beside him and show him from the Bible that although he had always felt an outcast, rejected and unloved, although his heart had been full of resentment and hatred, Jesus had paid the penalty for his crimes on the cross. And that even though he was now paralysed by fear of what lay beyond death Jesus could take away that fear and replace it with his peace if he could truly say he was sorry, repent, accept Christ as his Saviour and become a child of God with the promise of heaven at the end of his earthly journey.'

'On the Sunday morning,' Henry went on, 'two days before the date set for his execution, he knelt with me on the floor of his cell and accepted Jesus. And I think it was then that he understood that his fate, which until that moment he had resented and dreaded, was the fate of every human being. For we are all condemned to death from the minute we are born. But for those of us who believe in Jesus it is not the end but the realisation of an ultimate goal.

The next day when we met for the last time he was at peace, but he asked me to walk beside him as he went to the gallows. The Governor agreed and, at five o'clock that Tuesday morning, when I entered his cell he was peacefully sleeping.

'The astonished warder began shaking him.

'How can you lie there sleeping,' he cried, 'when you are to die in half an hour?'

'Why shouldn't I sleep?' he answered quietly. 'Jesus has given me his peace and I know I shall soon be with him: I've nothing to fear.'

'The warder was speechless,' Henry smiled, 'as the condemned man and I knelt and prayed together. Then he turned to me and said: "I'm ready."

'And as the dawn broke over our blue Bahaman sea we set off together on the short walk to the execution shed.'

'And that was the end?' I asked, my choked voice hardly above a whisper.

'That was the end,' Henry answered quietly. 'Or rather the beginning – the beginning of a new life for him, one without fear or rejection. Will you believe me if I say his face was radiant as he walked, not to the gallows – he saw beyond that, but to meet his Saviour?'

I nodded, unable to speak.

That evening as our plane hummed and began the climb which would take us across the short stretch of water to Miami, the sun was dipping into the gently lapping sea, tinting the horizon rose and mauve and apple green.

Yves and Christopher were already excitedly chattering about Florida, the Seaquarium, the Kennedy Space Centre, Disneyworld and all the other wonders which North America had in store for them.

But as we gained height and prepared to fly out into the sunset which had now cast itself like a shawl across those blue waters, I leaned forward and looked down at the fairytale island below. And beyond the rolling surf, the sun-drenched beaches, the gaily painted yachts and the colourful harbour I saw the roof of the prison: but above it hovered the memory of the Bahamas which I shall always carry with me, the radiant face of a man, forgiven, washed clean and born again, on the way to meet his God.

Chapter 7

A LOVE STORY

Not long after we returned home, and with this beautiful but poignant memory still fresh in my mind, I was telling the story to one of my friends, a woman in her sixties. I knew that she was very fearful of death but she was not prepared to accept Jesus as her Lord and Saviour and hand over her life into his hands because she was afraid of what he might ask her to give up if she did. For like the rich young man who wanted to follow Jesus but sadly turned away when our Lord said to him: 'Go, sell everything you have and give to the poor and you will have treasure in heaven' she had a great many of this world's possessions.

'It's not *when* one becomes a committed Christian which is important,' I explained. 'That prisoner committed his life to Jesus right at the last minute, just like the other criminal crucified on the cross next to Jesus who heard our Lord say: "Today you will be with me in Paradise".'

'Then that's easy,' my friend said lightly. 'I can go on living my life the way I want to and, just before I die, make a commitment to Jesus.'

It seemed simple, but I think that the next few words which God put on my heart shattered her.

'How do you know you are ever going to get up from that chair?' I enquired.

She looked across at me and blanched.

Her husband had died very suddenly one evening a few

years earlier just as he sat down to relax after a game of golf; one minute he was speaking to her and the next he was dead.

'We don't always have time,' I said quietly, 'you may leave it until it's too late. None of us knows when we are going to die and only God knows the exact hour.'

I think she saw the truth of the argument, although it did not at the time bring her to the foot of the cross. As Jesus said sadly to his disciples after the rich young man turned away: 'It is easier for a camel to go through the eye of a needle than for a rich man to enter the kingdom of God.'

And my friend is very rich.

But I hope that perhaps a seed was sown that day, that the words God gave me did not fall on stony ground and that she will come to realise that we none of us know what tomorrow will bring, even what the next hour or minute will bring. Tonight may be the end of the world for many, because death *is* the end of our world if we don't have eternal life to look forward to. And when the end comes, we may not have the time.

Our Lord means us to see his kingdom down here in our everyday life, and I began to wonder if I fail in my witness to those around me. I know I shall not convince them by insisting that I am right and everyone else is wrong, but only by showing them the truth through my shining example. And yet, how easily I get caught up in religiosity, so that what I tell people of Jesus doesn't seem to fit in with my own behaviour, as his child.

I can tell them what a difference knowing Jesus has made to my life. But if they don't see that difference? Then is it really there, or am I reciting a list of platitudes? It's so easy to fall into the rut of 'do as I say but not as I do', a rut out of which I frequently have to ruthlessly haul myself.

When I met Henry in Nassau it was obvious that he was 'different'. The love of God shone through him. And if we have really met Jesus and accepted him as our Lord and Saviour then this is what must happen and, when it does, it cannot help but show – those around us, those we bump into every day *must* see something different in us, and be drawn to him.

Henry must have been very simple when he lovingly presented his Saviour to that hardened criminal because the prisoner was not an educated man. But because the love of Jesus shone through Henry the prisoner was drawn, not to Henry, but to his Saviour. No earthly human power could have effected such a complete change in anyone, and brought him such peace. Only the Spirit of God flowing through Henry to touch the prisoner could have enabled him to be born again into a new life with Jesus.

It's not always easy to explain to someone who has not experienced it just what it means to be 'born again', to be liberated from our former self, delivered from our sins and set free to begin a new life with Jesus at the helm. And to begin this new life whilst we are still in our mortal bodies.

Nicodemus came to Jesus after dark one evening, fearing that the other members of the Sanhedrin would see him, and asked how he could obtain everlasting life.

'Unless a man is born again, he cannot see the kingdom of God,' Jesus answered.

Nicodemus was perplexed. He was an elderly, respected, learned member of Jewish society, but he was completely baffled by this unexpected statement.

'How can a man be born when he is old? Surely he cannot enter a second time into his mother's womb?' he asked incredulously.

Then Jesus explained it to him in these words: 'Flesh gives birth to flesh but the Spirit gives birth to Spirit.'

We are all born of water and of flesh in our natural human birth, but to be born again means to be born of the Spirit, our baptism of fire. This is what happened to the disciples at Pentecost after Jesus rose bodily into heaven to be with his Father. And it can happen to us today.

Before he ascended Jesus promised to send the apostles

another Comforter, the Holy Spirit: but a Comforter who would release his risen power in them and make them as strong and resistant as a fort, from which the word comforter stems. And on the Day of Pentecost his Holy Spirit, the third person of the Godhead, descended on the disciples. Onlookers said it was as if tongues of fire flamed down and danced above the head of each one of the twelve. They were given power, they began speaking in other tongues, they preached Jesus as Lord boldly and their lives were changed from that very moment. They were born again into a new dimension, a spiritual life as it is written, 'Therefore if anyone is in Christ, he is a new creature, the old has gone, the new has come.'

The most spectacular change was in the Apostle Peter who, when Jesus was taken away by the Roman soldiers on the night before his death and charged before Pontius Pilate with treason, had cowered in a corner of the courtyard afraid to look up and meet his master's eyes in case anyone should associate him with this man who would soon be condemned and crucified. And, as Jesus had told him he would, Peter had later that same night three times denied ever having known him.

But at Pentecost when the Holy Spirit came upon him, that once terrified coward who, later, had bitterly regretted his denial of his Lord, was suddenly transformed. Peter became bold and fearless and spent the rest of his life witnessing for Jesus, preaching the Gospel, in spite of threats from the authorities, knowing that his actions would certainly, in the end, lead to death. As indeed they did, the same death which Jesus had suffered and which Peter, before his new birth, had been so terrified even to be associated with.

This is what happens when we are born again.

We are liberated, freed to worship God, to enjoy his freedom because we have entered into a personal relationship with Jesus Christ. It is not a freedom to do what I like, but the freedom to do what is right. We have handed over our lives into God's hands, we have given up our 'right to ourselves' and entered into a relationship based entirely on trust; rather like the bond which exists between a mother and her child.

Jesus's freedom has nothing to do with the 'liberation' certain modern women are claiming which is an 'I' freedom, putting 'me' first.

Jesus's freedom doesn't put me first, it is like the freedom a baby must enjoy when he is held tightly in his mother's arms. Only then can he kick and stretch and bounce up and down and throw back his head and laugh. The baby is free to move in every direction because he knows that someone he loves and trusts is holding him tightly, and will not allow him to come to any harm.

And this is the only true freedom because, when we accept it, we are no longer under the law. As we receive the Holy Spirit we also receive the fruits of the Spirit listed in Galatians: love, joy, peace, patience, kindness, goodness, gentleness, faithfulness, self-control, against which there is no law. If we live according to the fruits of the Spirit we are not law-less but law-free. Have you ever heard of a law forbidding these nine virtues?

But until we become 'law-free' we are all slaves, clinging to our lives. It is only the person who gives up his life into God's safekeeping, trusting him to lead him, who is truly free for, contrary to man's rule, surrender to God means freedom.

And when we have this wonderful freedom, this precious gift, we want to share it with others; we can't keep it a secret, hug it to ourselves. It's like falling in love.

When you fell in love can't you remember how your heart seemed to be bursting with happiness? Everything looked different, even the rain or the cold or a stormy day didn't matter; life was suddenly beautiful and all its colour heightened. The grass was greener, the sky looked bluer, the flowers more scented, the birds sang more sweetly, and even if it snowed it was whiter, crisper, purer, one didn't notice the slush. That's how I felt when I finally gave in and accepted

Jesus. As I looked up through my tears of joy, everything was the same, nothing outwardly had changed, but my heart had changed. And that made all the difference.

When your husband asked you to spend the rest of your earthly life with him, didn't you want to rush out and tell this wonderful news to the first person you met and, even more, share your happiness with those dearest to you? I know I did. And I remember the glorious moment of waking each morning to a world which was sparkling and I couldn't wait for the moment when we would be together again. Life suddenly took on another dimension when I found that very special person to whom I could willingly give my heart and my life – all else faded into the background.

When you meet Jesus, a love story begins. But the wonder of his love is that it is not fragile like earthly love, there is not a vestige of selfishness in it, it is an unconditional love with no strings attached, a love which does not change or wear thin with time. And it is immortal, for it says in Romans: 'Who shall separate us from the love of Christ?' and goes on to say that neither hardship, persecution nor death can do so.

Even in the most perfect of earthly marriages we know that one day one of us will be left to face life alone. That precious bond, if we are Christians, will only temporarily be cut by death, but it will be cut and, as we grow older, we see it happening to our friends.

But the Bible says: 'Perfect love drives out fear'.

Only God's love is perfect and without fear, not subject to sickness or ageing bones, and our freedom to truly love another person can only flow from a deep certainty of him.

How I wish I had truly known him when I married.

How grateful I am that I know him now. And how my heart aches for my grandmother, who went almost to the end of her life without him, though I am convinced that we can never be entirely sure that anyone dies without being given one last chance of coming face to face with their Saviour.

Grannie, the delicate one of her family, who had always

been spoilt and coddled by everyone all her life survived her five sisters, which must have been traumatic for her. For, although she would never have admitted it, she relied on them so much, especially Great-Aunt Jessica.

My grandmother remained very domineering and lucid right to the end, though at times after Aunt Jessica's death, she tended to wander off and live in a world of her own. I remember one Christmas Day not long after the Queen came to the throne – she must still have been in her twenties at the time, and Grannie was approaching ninety – we were all gathered in front of the television set after lunch to hear the Queen's traditional speech.

Grannie was sitting erect and dignified in a chair and I was on a pouf at her feet. She was a little bewildered by the television and didn't entirely 'hold with it', tending to voice her opinions loudly and talk her way through most programmes. And she prepared to do just that as the young Queen's picture was flashed on to the screen.

I remember laying a restraining hand on her arm and saying, 'Hush Grannie and listen, it won't be long. That's the Queen speaking.'

'The Queen,' Grannie replied regally, picking up the pince-nez hanging from the chain around her neck and adjusting it so that she could see more clearly.

'Indeed,' she said reverently, letting the chain drop back to her chest. 'She *does* carry her age well.'

For the moment Grannie had slipped back in time. Perhaps family Christmases encourage this nostalgic going back down the years, recalling the 'good old days' which weren't always as good as we like to imagine. And the young Queen on the television screen, in my grandmother's mind, was the widowed Victoria she had known in her youth.

My grandmother died just before her ninety-first birthday. She might well have lived to be a hundred had she not slipped and fallen, breaking her hip. The operation to repair the damaged bone was successful but when, as so often happens with people of great age, she developed hyopostatic pneumonia, mercifully she was not hooked up to all kinds of apparatus which she would have loathed, but allowed to die with dignity.

I feel sure that in those last days, as she lay weak and helpless in the hospital bed, Jesus came and spoke to her, opening the gates of heaven and offering her his precious gift of eternal life.

Only he could have changed my beloved Grannie who had always been so autocratic, so demanding and so afraid of death, and enabled her to meet it humbly and serenely. She, who had always been far too proud ever to admit that she was wrong or to apologise, who had never shown any of us physical affection, held my mother's hand in hers as she lay dying and asked her daughter's forgiveness for the pain she had caused her.

To her grandchildren she had been a gay, fascinating, amusing grandmother, but she had never been a loving mother. She had even boasted that, despite the nurses pleas, she had refused to look at my mother, her first-born, for five days because she had hoped for a son. Yet, as she lay dying, my grandmother gazed up at her elder daughter with a gentleness my mother had never seen before in her still beautiful slate-blue eyes and said quietly.

'You've been a good girl to me Nora, all your life, and I've never appreciated it. I'm sorry for the hurt I've caused you and I want you to know how much your love has meant to me.'

My mother was then in her mid-sixties, but perhaps to Grannie she was still a little girl, a little girl who so needed her mother's love and had never really received it. I know that she was deeply moved by her mother's dying words and that they completely wiped away the memory of the lack of love and the many hurts my mother had received from Grannie's tongue over the years.

It wasn't my grandmother speaking like that. Not the

grandmother we knew. Only the love of Jesus and his Holy Spirit filling her heart could have enabled her to humble herself and ask her daughter's forgiveness. Humility is one of the signs of a truly committed Christian and it was a virtue Grannie had never possessed. Rather the opposite.

But those dying words make me sure that she has eternal life, that Jesus came to her with his precious gift in those last days, as he did to the condemned man in the Nassau gaol.

It may appear to some to be unfair that she should, in the end, be granted forgiveness and have the doors of heaven opened to her.

The Bible tells us in the parable of the workers in the vineyard that those who worked all day received the same wages as those who were only hired in the evening. That doesn't seem fair either, does it? Perhaps not when one looks at it superficially, but with the dreadful unemployment rampant in Europe in these closing years of the twentieth century this parable is particularly topical. When one thinks about it, it makes its point very clearly, showing that those who had worked all day had the security, the satisfaction and the dignity of work, whereas those who had only been hired at the last minute had spent the day in uncertainty and doubt, not knowing whether they were going to be hired at all, only knowing the misery and degradation of hanging around waiting for work.

We who accept this gift God offers us early in life – or in the day, to pinpoint the parable – have the joy of walking with Jesus throughout our lives. But those who, like my grandmother and the condemned prisoner, only discover their Saviour at the last minute have spent all those years without any certainty of salvation, without the peace and hope and security which a daily walk with Jesus brings.

Who knows how different that prisoner's life might have been had Henry met him and witnessed to him years before? I am sure it was not in God's plan for his life that that man should die on the gallows! For we read in the book of

Lamentations: 'He does not willingly bring affliction or grief to the children of men.' God only wants good for his children but he has given us free will to make our own choice, knowing full well what it will cost him. As it says in Deuteronomy, another old Testament book, 'See I set before you today life and prosperity, death and destruction'. We only have two choices, good or evil, heaven or hell, and so many people imagine that hell is going to be as amusing as the road which leads up to it: how our Lord's heart must bleed for them.

Chapter 8

NOT THE GARDENER

I wish my grandmother had met Jesus eighty or even seventy or sixty years before. I am sure that she would have had a much more contented, fulfilled life, certainly a life without the guilt and fears which haunted her and probably made her as she was. She had such a short time to experience his peace here on earth before she came face to face with him in heaven.

Maybe he had come to her before, as he comes to each one of us during the course of our lives, and asks us to let him come into our hearts. But sometimes I think he comes and we don't recognise him. Perhaps we are not entirely to be blamed for that either for, after his crucifixion when he stepped in beside two of his disciples and walked with them along the road to Emmaus, even they did not recognise him. It was only when they offered him hospitality for the night and, at supper, he took the bread and broke it, giving thanks, that the realisation of who he was struck them. Then they saw again the upper room where, on the night before he died he had done the same thing and pronounced the words: 'This is my body given for you, do this in remembrance of me.' Only then, as the truth dawned on them, did they fall at his feet in worship and adoration.

The same thing happened when Mary Magdalene went to the tomb early on that first Easter morning with spices to embalm Jesus's body. As she stood there, grief-stricken at finding the stone rolled away and the tomb empty, Jesus appeared beside her. But even she did not recognise him: she thought he was the gardener. And, once again, it was only when he spoke to her, said 'Miriam', calling her by her familiar name, that the light dawned and she fell sobbing at his feet.

So perhaps it's not altogether surprising that when we are seeking the truth we don't always immediately recognise him either. Like Mary Magdalene and the disciples we think of him as dead. So that when he does come to us in his risen power, our finite minds cannot take in the enormity of what is happening. We cannot believe it and often we run away. But when we do take time to wait, to pause, to listen, he calls us by name, as he did Mary Magdalene, and we suddenly realise that what the Bible says is true: Jesus DID rise again, he IS alive and he is here with us now, our living Lord and Saviour.

Doubtless many people are like I was. I didn't immediately recognise him because I was bogged down with all sorts of preconceived ideas of what it meant to be a Christian. I thought I had to be worthy, I didn't realise that nobody is ever worthy.

I also imagined that my meeting with him had to be spectacular, that when I fell at his feet, like the wise men, I had to bring him costly gifts. But the only gift he asks us to bring is ourselves.

We hear the Christmas story and we read in the New Testament about the shepherds in the fields being awakened by a blazing light and seeing angels, hearing them singing and telling the shepherds to follow the star to the stable where Jesus was lying in a manger – that star which the astronomers had heard of and been searching the night sky for for years. When it finally appeared the three wise men set out on their camels bearing costly gifts and followed it till it led them to where the baby Jesus lay.

Perhaps we are waiting till we hear the angels singing, telling us where to go to find him. Perhaps, like the wise men on that first Christmas night, we are waiting for the star to guide us, and we worry because we have no costly gifts to bring, no gold, no frankincense or myrrh.

Maybe when Jesus comes to us we will hear angels singing, maybe we will see a bright star in the east, but I think it unlikely. My grandmother may have thought that she had to come with costly gifts, had to be someone special. I don't know. I only know that I was forty years old, weak and broken when I met him; I was no one special, and my hands were empty. As the old well-loved hymn says: 'Nothing in my hands I bring, simply to thy cross I cling.'

Jesus came to me at a time in my life when I had nothing to give him but my sin, and only his cross to cling to, and it was then that he bent down and held out his hand and lifted me up. For didn't the Psalmist say of the Lord: 'a broken and a contrite heart, O God, you will not despise'.

He had been knocking at the door of my heart for a very long time, I realise that now, but I hadn't heard him till then. I'd been too busy, too obsessed with the world and its pleasures, its worries, its distractions, hustle and bustle on every side of me, my days filled with things of so little importance which had assumed such magnitude in my life. And, as my material possessions expanded, so my senses began to diminish and my heart contract.

Mercifully my foot slipped before it was too late and I found myself in a world of mental and spiritual darkness, flat on my back, down at the bottom of that deep black pit with unscalable sides and nothing but night all around me. And there where time had ceased to have any meaning and material possessions any importance, where there was nothing left to hope for I looked up. When you have reached the very depths, there's nowhere else to look. And I met my Saviour face to face.

In the Psalms David said: 'Out of the depths I cry to you, O Lord; O Lord hear my voice'.

From the recesses of my childhood memories, from my Sunday School days those words came back to me down in that black pit of guilt, depression and self-pity, and I cried out to Jesus without any real conviction that he would hear me or that he was even there. But Jesus is always there, waiting to meet us at the point of our deepest need, and I thank my God for taking me down into the depths. Would I ever have found him otherwise?

I can be still now. I don't have to keep rushing, for Jesus has given my life a purpose and a meaning: he has given me his peace. He has not handed me a detailed map showing me exactly where he is leading me, where we are going to pause and rest, where there will be steep mountains and deep valleys. No, mercifully, he spares us knowledge of the future and tells us to live each day to the full, as it comes and leave tomorrow in his hands. But he does promise that, wherever he leads he will be there beside us, that he will never leave us or forsake us, and that all we have is safe in his hands.

And, as he gave me that assurance, I realised that God does not work through methods and machines but through people, all those thousands of people both dear and unknown who cross the path of our lives. And that sometimes he chooses the most unlikely people to fulfil his purposes and show us ourselves as he sees us, and not as we like to think we are. He doesn't point out our faults as much as show them to us through those he brings into our lives, often people whom we fail. People who would perhaps have responded to real love, as in the end they always do, if only we had taken the time and had the courage to show it to them.

Pierrot was one of those people.

Chapter 9

WHERE IS PIERROT?

I first met Pierrot on a drizzly February afternoon. My husband's aunt had died and, as the funeral procession was crossing our sodden garden, he appeared round the side of the house and stood there, head bowed, as her coffin passed.

Tante Lucie had always had a tremendous sense of humour and would have laughed heartily had she seen him, his tattered felt hat held respectfully across his chest, stray wisps of damp, matted beard escaping round the edges, and a birch twig broom clutched stiffly to attention in his free hand.

Pierrot reappeared with the changing seasons from then onwards and always reverently referred to our first meeting. He kept us supplied with brooms to sweep the lawn; was always courteous, humorous, cheerful and philosophical; and the children loved him. Sometimes there were longer gaps than usual between his visits.

''Fraid I've been in hospital again, madame,' he would explain on his next appearance. 'Usual old problem.'

And he would tap his chest and give an apologetic cough.

I always sympathised with him and longed to help, for I knew it was not a bronchial problem which had kept him away, but the results of a skirmish with the police after a longer than usual bout with the bottle. But I also knew that any reference to the real cause would mean the end of our relationship.

Pierrot was well known to everyone, but without any of us really 'knowing' him. He was a loner, a true 'non-conformist', the black sheep of one of the local families which had now moved away and scattered. The older inhabitants of our village, most of whom had grown up with him, treated him in a friendly enough fashion, but with a mixture of humour and condescension which on the surface, left him unmoved. No one knew where he now lived and when I asked him he merely smiled and waved his hand towards the forest, towards those dark, cool glades where, at dawn, young deer could be glimpsed plunging through the leaves and, at twilight, baby rabbits played.

He was one of those rare, free spirits who did not want to be hampered by work or ties of any kind, so I respected his independence. But this apparent misfit in our society had an attraction and a sweetness which the children found irresistible and sometimes on dark, stormy nights one of them would awaken and say:

'Mummie, I wonder where Pierrot is?'

And I could not comfort them. I didn't know.

As the years went by he called on us socially, no longer with a birch broom as an excuse for his seasonal visits. He would rarely have anything to eat when he came but, after our little chat about life and village events, always accepted with great dignity the money I slipped into his hand. But, as time went on, although his drinking was never offensive, his taste for red wine imprisoned him.

The last time I saw him, one bright frosty morning in early December, his shoes were flapping at the uppers. He tried on an almost new pair of outgrown wellington boots, deep green like his forest, which I dug out for him, and they fitted him perfectly. He was delighted. He looked much thinner and older that day, almost ethereal in fact, and his flowing beard was streaked with white.

My heart went out to him and, for once, I broke our unspoken pact:

'You've lost weight,' I said quietly . . . and waited for him to tell me more.

'I'm afraid I spent the last month in hospital madame,' he answered politely. 'I'm not quite back on my feet again yet.'

I knew that he considered the subject closed, so I played his game, afraid that if I attempted to pry further I would frighten him away completely.

As he turned to leave, although I knew where it would go, I pressed some money into his hand. Perhaps I was mistaken but, as he said goodbye, I thought I saw tears in his eyes and, on an impulse, almost ran after that slight, stooping figure as he walked slowly down the path.

I felt a sudden urgency. I wanted to finally break down the invisible barrier which had always lain between us, the barrier he had himself erected and ask him: 'Who are you, where have you come from, what happened years ago to turn you away from the world, from the comfortable life which must once have been yours?'

His speech was cultured, his voice soft and modulated and, despite his threadbare clothes, he had an air about him, an old-world courtesy which intrigued me.

But above all I wanted to tell him about Jesus. Yet I held back.

As if he read my thoughts he turned and, with an incredibly sweet smile on his face, raised his tattered felt hat and bowed low in a gracious, old-fashioned salute. Then he walked through the gate and was gone.

Christmas came and went and the hard winter which had been forecast set in almost before we had taken down the decorations. The cold was biting and, as day after day the snowflakes drifted silently past the window to bury themselves in the vast white sea below, Pierrot would come into my thoughts and I would see again that sweet, enigmatic smile, the tattered hat raised in salute and the unanswered questions would crowd in and tantalise my mind.

We had begun to think that spring would never come

when, suddenly, the snow disappeared and crocuses and tulips started to peep through the dark, damp soil. Easter was early that year and, as the days lengthened and the morning birdsong increased, I wondered why Pierrot didn't appear on the doorstep as usual. He had come to symbolise something for me, something I subconsciously looked for and could count on, like the changing seasons.

Then one golden April morning I stopped on my way to the market to give a lift to 'Grande-Mère', who has been scrubbing for the local families for the last fifty years. She looked at me reproachfully when I asked if she'd seen Pierrot.

'But, madame,' she exclaimed, 'didn't you hear what happened?'

I hadn't heard anything that winter, cocooned as I was in my sheltered warmth.

'He fell asleep by the fire he'd made in his forest shack and his rubber boots caught alight,' she went on. 'The gamekeeper heard him calling two days later, but by that time both feet had gone gangrenous and had to be amputated.'

She stopped and looked away from me, through the car window at nothing in particular.

'He died in the hospital on New Year's Eve,' she ended laconically.

I slowed the car to a standstill in front of the noisy, crowded market. The gaily striped awnings over the stalls piled high with shining, multicoloured fruit and vegetables contrasted strangely with the sudden drabness I felt. Neither Grande-Mère nor I spoke. We both knew that with Pierrot's death something infinitely sweet had gone from our midst and a page had turned on an era of our village life.

The old lady sighed and, picking up her wicker basket, heaved herself out of the car.

I didn't ask her where he was buried. I already knew. In that large, unadorned patch of our heavily ornamented cemetery reserved for those 'without means' – the paupers' grave. I would have liked to have gone with him on that last short walk and thrown some wild flowers or even a few branches from his forest home into that barren grave. But Pierrot left our village as he had lived in it – alone – and he took his secret with him.

On that sparkling April morning I knew that now I would never have the answers to those questions I had almost asked on that cold December day. I would never know why a life which had obviously begun so differently should end in a communal, unmarked grave. But what hurt most of all was the knowledge that I would never now have the chance to introduce him to Jesus; that I had failed my Lord and had not gone into the world and preached the Gospel to all peoples as he told us to do.

The world Jesus was talking about was my own little world, my village, and 'all peoples, all nations,' were my neighbours, the people I came in contact with every day and ... Pierrot, that sweet, sad, lonely spirit who so needed love and yet who, for reasons I had not bothered to discover, shied away from it.

Like most people I hadn't realised the urgency. And yet hadn't I preached urgency to my rich friend? How could I have thought that there was plenty of time when Jesus had warned us that 'the Son of Man will come at an hour when you do not expect him.' How often we preach to others and yet, as I did, still that insistent small voice inside us saying it isn't the moment, there will be another 'more suitable' occasion. But for Pierrot there hadn't been.

I learned from bitter experience that none of us can ever be sure that there will be another occasion. This one we are facing today may well be our last chance to share Jesus with a lost soul, with someone who sorely needs him.

When I got back home that morning I brought my sorrow and my guilt for what had happened before Jesus in prayer and I had the feeling that he was saying to me what he had once said to his disciples: 'How long must I put up with you?' In other words: will you never learn! Sometimes I think I must have driven my Saviour to the end of his tether. But although he chided me I knew that he was chiding me in love and saying, as he had said to the woman he had saved from stoning, 'Go now and leave your life of sin'.

For I am convinced that it is a sin to keep silent, to hide this wonderful news of salvation from those who are seeking, who are hungry for the meaning of life. And almost everyone IS seeking, they may not admit it or even realise it but, if they haven't found the one true God, then they will create one for themselves.

In this materialistic age we see such 'gods' all around us: fame, success, money, possessions, to mention only a few. They all guarantee us everything but happiness and are passports to everywhere but heaven – and they can all crumble and fade away in the twinkling of an eye. As Jesus warned us, they can give us no lasting guarantee of security however much we worship them, for there is only one God who is worthy of our praise and adoration, who will never let us down, who is as firm and solid as a rock and whose love is everlasting. And yet how often we who have met him and tested his strength, known his peace and love, do not share it with those who are hungry for him, who are worshipping false gods. How often do we fail in our task?

And here I stand accused.

Whenever we realise that we have failed to do something when the perfect opportunity has been offered to us, we tend first of all to sink into despair and then make excuses, or at least I did. The devil specialises in making them to measure for us and, in my remorse, I busied myself firing the ammunition he prepared. But when I stopped the volley, the reality was still there. I had failed. It was a lesson I learned the hard way.

Yet as I prayed it was as if Jesus said: 'the past is gone, that door is closed and will never be reopened, that opportunity is lost forever: you cannot alter it. But never let the overwhelming sense of failure cloud and corrupt your future:

get up, look ahead and go forward to the next thing I have prepared for you, the next lost child I will put across your path. Let the past lie buried, but buried with me.'

So I got up from my knees and, as King David did after his baby son died, washed my face and went humbly forward. I could only pray that in the solitude of that forest glade where Pierrot had hidden himself and his secret, Jesus, who looks into each heart and sees its hurts and its longings, had come to him, as I know he came to my grandmother so many years before.

They were so different: Grannie so proud, so autocratic and demanding. Pierrot so sweet, humble and ethereal. And yet they both had the same deep hidden needs – of Jesus and his love.

My consolation was that death is the great leveller and that those with no place in this world are so often recognised and acknowledged by Jesus. As Job said, 'naked I came from my mother's womb and naked I shall depart.' Pierrot was now equal with all those who had gone before him.

Chapter 10

THE HUB OF THE WHEEL

What a responsibility we have as mothers, and an even greater one as Christian mothers. It's up to us not only to set the tone of the home, be the hub around which the wheel of the family revolves but also, together with our husbands, to obey God's instructions and 'bring our children up in the way they should go'.

So many people's happiness depends on us, not only their physical well-being but their inner happiness as well, because when Mum is grumpy or bad tempered then the rest of the family tends to follow suit.

My mother's remark to her cousin Sybil all those years ago about her family being her most important guests has often pulled me up sharply when I've tended to think that my family can do with the odd pieces, even the scraps of my affection or the ragged end of my smile, or when I have let family life become the battlefield for all my frustrations of the day, keeping my smiling face for guests.

And yet the wonderful thing about a family, or so I've found, is that I don't have to put on a front or always be on my best behaviour, they accept me as I am. And children, especially young children, are so loving and forgiving.

I've discovered that Jesus is like that too.

He accepts us just as we are and, since I came to know him as my friend and Saviour and began trying to be his missionary to my family, I have 'found myself' – as the media

is always urging modern women to do. I have fulfilled myself
– another favourite phrase of theirs – in watching the children
grow to adulthood and become 'themselves'. Like so many
things in life, when we stop seeking personal fulfilment, it
comes naturally through the happiness we bring to others.

For didn't Jesus say: 'whatever you did for one of the least
of these brothers of mine, you did for me'.

What a privilege! In loving, in caring for, and in 'giving
ourselves' to our growing families, we women who choose to
play the old-fashioned role, and become 'just housewives' are
not only ministering to those nearest and dearest to us but we
are ministering to Jesus as well.

And yet it's not always easy, is it? Especially today when
everything shrieks at a woman to 'liberate' herself. From
what, I sometimes wonder? Sometimes all the 'liberation'
amounts to, for a married woman, is carrying a double load.

But it's easy to get unnerved by all this feminist publicity
and begin to query the path we've chosen, wonder just where
it's leading, even whether it's worth it. We ask ourselves why
we are spending our days doing mundane tasks which will all
have to be done again tomorrow, running round in endless
circles being cook, nurse, housekeeper, governess, hostess,
playmate and chauffeur to a family who, so often, take it all
for granted and don't appear to notice we're even there,
leaving us with the feeling that our brain is slowly shrivelling
up for want of exercise. Especially when the children are
young and there is so little adult company and our
conversation seems to consist of 'not now dear', 'don't do
that', 'let him have it, he's younger than you', 'I'll read you a
story when I've finished washing up, making the beds, peeling
the potatoes, bathing the baby, dressing the toddler, clearing
up the mess'. I know I used to, especially on a wet Monday
morning as I stared hopelessly at the weekend debris, and
wondered where on earth to begin.

It's so easy at such times to fall into a well of self-pity.
There's not only the fatigue of constantly looking after small

children, but also the media whispering incessantly in our ears that being a wife and mother is the job of a second-class citizen.

But Jesus doesn't consider us like that.

Has it ever struck you that Jesus was perhaps the only person two thousand years ago, when male dominance was supreme and women had no status at all, to stand up for the rights of women? He didn't consider them inferior, even though he laid down rules for family living putting the husband as head of the house, but under God.

It may not have occurred to you either that the first person to whom Jesus revealed himself on that resurrection Easter morning was a woman. It wasn't to one of his disciples, it wasn't to the High Priest or Nicodemus or Pontius Pilate; it wasn't to anyone important, but to Mary Magdalene, a very ordinary, humble woman. A woman who would have been shunned and looked down upon by the people of her day, and possibly even by the 'respectable' citizens of our day. Yet she was the one Jesus chose to announce to his sorrowing disciples the news of their master's resurrection ... *her* name is remembered two thousand years later when many 'big names', important people of the time, have long since been forgotten.

I think housewives have a very special relationship with Jesus. Remember how he loved those home makers Martha and Mary? It was to their house he came for refreshment and peace after long hours of teaching and preaching and days on the dusty road. Theirs was perhaps the only real home he knew, after he left his carpenter's shop in Nazareth to do his heavenly Father's will.

And didn't he say: 'Take my yoke upon you and learn from me, for I am gentle and humble in heart, and you will find rest for your souls. For my yoke is easy and my burden is light'.

Those words weren't aimed especially at women, they were and are for everyone. But to me they are particularly relevant for the tired, overworked housewife; they are wonderful words for the harassed young mother to hear.

Being yoked with Jesus means walking in step with him along the furrow he is tracing for our lives, with him sharing the load. He says in effect 'get alongside me and we will pull together'. And when we agree to hand over our heavy load, when we trust him to lead us, we become his children. Children of the King.

It took me some time to really grasp that.

I am a daughter of the King, and a much-loved daughter at that.

We don't have to be intelligent or beautiful, or from a privileged race or class to be his beloved child: we only have to believe. God's Word says: 'To those who believed in his name, he gave the right to become the children of God.'

When we understand this it makes so many things just fall away. All the pettiness, the snobbery, the self-importance, the striving for power, the resentments. If we are children of the King, no matter what the media or anyone else says, we cannot be second-class citizens.

As I grasped the full significance of this fact one of the most amazing revelations of God came to me: that it is not in the visions but in the everyday things, the drudgery even that we find him; that the deity of Jesus is understood when we cheerfully tackle the particular job he has given us for that moment. And as this knowledge seeped through me I stopped trying to justify myself in the eyes of friends who were rushing about doing glamorous jobs. I accepted my role, and the great responsibility attached to it, of shaping and forming the next generation, of trying to create a home which was really a home, a haven where the disappointments and frustrations, the problems and the injustices of the day could be fought out in a loving atmosphere. A home where the children could work through their rebellious period, and all five of them did, in an atmosphere of love and acceptance, instead of having to fight their battles for identity in an outside world which almost certainly would not have accepted them as they were and loved them in spite of it.

Chapter 11

MY PEACE I GIVE YOU

But in order to live through these difficult times, even as children of the King, we need that special gift which Jesus promised to his disciples before he left them.

'Peace I leave with you,' he said, 'my peace I give you. I do not give to you as the world gives. Do not let your hearts be troubled, and do not be afraid.'

The world can give us a kind of peace, but it is so often a peace based on ignorance which only lasts until we awaken to the facts. True, lasting, unshakable peace is only to be found in Jesus and it comes when we stop the hurly-burly, the frantic rush of modern life, and look into his face, drink in his tranquillity.

Why are we always in such a hurry nowadays? Why do we never have any time? Jesus never hurried, he always had time. And what peace, what serenity he had.

It's this peace which every mother needs so that she can pass it on to her family, a haven of peace in a tension-ridden world, a peace which the world certainly cannot give her.

As Jesus promised, I received it immediately I accepted him. It flowed through me like a wonderful cleansing stream and I thought that I would float along on this caressing tide for the rest of my life, never knowing another storm or an angry sea.

But I was young in the faith and, as so often happens when we come off the crest of the wave, after having met Jesus, the tired old world comes seeping back into our lives and we sometimes forget that we are children of the almighty King.

It happened to me and I began to have doubts and become disillusioned. I remember sulkily telling my Lord one morning that I had given my life into his safe-keeping and received only problems in return . . . or so it appeared to me at the time. And it was then that he led me to an exhibition of painting.

My young cousin was staying with us at the time. I was seventeen years his senior and, remembering the distance not only in years but in every other way, which had once separated Sybil and me, I heeded the warning and, in consequence, my attitude towards Brian was relaxed and friendly. Quite the opposite of what Sybil's attitude to me, as a child, had been. I had always greatly enjoyed this young cousin, and even more so as he grew older and came over to France to stay with us for holidays.

'Come on,' I remember saying to him that warm September afternoon, 'all I've ever done is take you up the Eiffel Tower. It's time you had some culture. This afternoon we're going to a painting exhibition.'

Brian had grimaced. He would most probably have much preferred the swimming pool, but he was a good-natured youth and always fell in easily with any suggestion.

Normally I would have taken him on some other outing. I enjoy art but it would have been more appropriate to have introduced Brian to the Louvre, shown him the really great masters or visited the Jeu de Paume where the Impressionists are housed. This local exhibition wasn't anything special; in fact it was a painting competition. And yet I felt compelled to go.

The subject was peace.

There were some really lovely entries, ones I would have been happy to have in my home. Lots of leafy lanes in summer and rainbow sunsets over tranquil blue seas: lots of dream cottages with rambler roses climbing round the door and old-world gardens full of sweet-peas and foxgloves. Yet, strangely enough, it wasn't one of those which won the prize. And it certainly wasn't one which I would have chosen to hang on my wall.

The winning entry showed a storm at sea.

There, under a leaden sky huge grey waves were hurtling ten feet into the air and dashing with tremendous force against a steep cliff. The picture was terrifying at first glance: one could almost hear the roar as each angry wave rose menacingly, white froth boiling on its tip as it prepared to crash.

I remember staring in astonishment at the painting as we came up to it.

'What on earth has that to do with peace?' I enquired as we peered in amazement at the winning entry, trying to find an explanation.

'Not much,' Brian grimaced. 'It's *anything* but peaceful.'

And, shaking our heads in bewilderment, we prepared to pass on to the next entry.

Brian had already moved along, but something held me back and I stood rooted in front of the canvas, gazing at the frothing sea. As I took a closer look, high above the waves near the top of the cliff face I noticed a crevice in the rock and in it, tucked away from the wind and the storm, was a large bird, perched on a nest, her wings spread to protect the chicks inside.

Seeing that great bird impassively watching the raging sea, waiting for the storm to pass, made me think of Jesus asleep in the boat tossing on the angry waves of Lake Galilee. His disciples had been terrified and woke him up, fearing they would all be drowned.

'Peace, be still,' Jesus said.

And the storm subsided.

Then he rebuked his disciples for their lack of trust.

I knew then why I had been drawn to this particular exhibition when there were so many other more impressive, more beautiful and more famous works of art to be seen in Paris. Jesus had led me there in order to show me how easy it is for our trust in him to fail when the storm rages round our personal cliff face. My cliff face was steep at that time, and the storm was raging round it wildly but, having met Jesus, I had felt let down when after the first euphoria I came back to earth and realised that all my problems weren't going to be taken away from me, or immediately solved, and my life become a bed of roses from then on.

'It's easy to trust and believe in me when you're at peace and things are going well, isn't it?' Jesus had said as I stood rooted to the spot, still gazing up at the picture.

'But when they're not?' he continued.

And I knew what he meant.

As I had done when I married, I had placed my hand in his for better or for worse, and now that the worst seemed to be happening I was rebelling, feeling sorry for myself and wanting to know why. I had forgotten, or perhaps at that time I didn't really believe, that if there is a force for good in the world, there is also a force for evil and, knowing that he had lost me to Jesus, the devil was having a last ditch stand to get me back into his camp. I had also forgotten that Satan is a defeated enemy. Jesus conquered him and diffused his power over us once and for all when he died on the cross. And, as the Bible tells us, our Lord doesn't change for 'Jesus Christ is the same yesterday, today and for ever'. We may change, but he doesn't.

'You can trust me,' Jesus said gently, 'and have peace in the midst of the storm even in this restless world of today.'

And in that moment I reached a little further along the path of my Christian walk when, standing in front of that storm-tossed picture, I turned and said to Jesus: 'I believe you, Lord.'

And, as I did so, the deep peace which I had known when I first came to him and which, in the turmoil of daily living, in the midst of my problems, which I had been trying to solve in my own strength, I had lost slowly returned and flooded my whole being once again. And I knew that what Jesus promises he fulfils. That even if I was, like that bird, in the midst of a raging storm, like the bird I could look out calmly and impassively at the roaring waves, because having Jesus in my life made all the difference.

Our Lord promised his disciples that peace which the world cannot give. The world couldn't give people peace two thousand years ago and it can't give us peace today. But Jesus's promise still holds, and so does his peace; that peace which the Apostle Paul wrote about when he was in chains in a dark, damp Roman prison. An unlikely place to have peace, yet he had it and he rejoiced and praised God for it.

He had it throughout all the storms of his life, and they were many. He even had it when the boat taking him to Rome for trial was shipwrecked. Everyone around him was terrified and his guards suggested throwing him overboard in order to save their own skins. But Paul still had peace, because he knew the one in whom he had put his trust – the friend and Saviour who would not fail him.

As Jesus brought all these images back to my mind while I stood gazing at that stormy picture, he showed me that the peace he offers is, in a way, the same peace which that bird had when she sat on her nest above the roaring waves, knowing she was safe and out of their range. It is something we have deep inside us, whether the sky is blue or grey, whether our sea is smooth or raging.

'Be like that eagle sitting impassively on her nest above the roaring waves,' Jesus said.

I hadn't been aware that it was an eagle, but at that moment favourite lines from Isaiah came into my mind. I was not over-familiar with the Bible at that time, but I was groping and finding my way through it and certain passages, especially those dealing with weariness, had impressed themselves on my mind.

'Those who hope in the Lord will renew their strength.

They will soar on wings like eagles, they will run and not grow weary, they will walk and not be faint'.

I liked the idea of rising up.

'Be like the eagle,' Jesus said again. 'He never fights the elements, he never frantically flaps his wings against the currents, he just waits until the moment is favourable then spreads his wings, rises up and rides the winds, letting the current carry him through. He waits, rises and floats; with me beside you you can do the same.'

I hadn't realised that the eagle never flapped his wings. I hadn't realised that it never went against the wind but allowed itself to be carried along by it. Maybe the artist who painted the picture knew all this; maybe he or she was even a Christian trying to convey a message to the public. I don't know.

Brian's voice broke in on my dreaming.

'There you are,' he exclaimed coming to a standstill beside me. 'I thought I'd lost you.'

I smiled up at him.

'What's happened to you?' my cousin laughed. 'You look moonstruck.'

'Not really,' I joined in his laughter. 'But the picture fascinated me and the more I looked at it, the more I read into it.'

Brian glanced up at it and away again.

'Looks pretty grim to me,' he observed, 'don't think I want to buy it for my bedroom wall.'

'Yes,' I mused as we turned to go, 'I suppose as the world sees it the winning entry *is* an unusual picture, not what anyone would expect from a subject like peace.'

I glanced longingly back at it as we turned and walked away. I was grateful for what it had taught me, the depths it had revealed to me, and felt at that moment that I wouldn't in the least mind hanging it on my bedroom wall. It could keep me buoyant in difficult moments, keep me soaring, my eyes looking to Jesus.

'But I can see what caught the judge's attention,' I said as we walked towards the exit. 'Why it won the prize.'

Brian glanced down at me, surprise showing in his brown eyes.

'It reminded me of the Christian life,' I said simply.

My young cousin made no comment as we walked in silence out into the sunny street. It was time to go back to the car and return home before the children came tumbling in from school, so I said nothing more. Perhaps it wasn't the right moment to witness to him, I don't know. I only know that Brian was not a committed Christian at that time, although he had been faithfully taken to church by his parents throughout his young life. I do know that he is committed now and it has created an even deeper bond between us.

Chapter 12

GENERATION AFTER GENERATION

One golden autumn afternoon not long after visiting the painting exhibition, I was alone in the kitchen making jam. The memory of those precious moments spent with Jesus in the quiet gallery had remained with me and sustained me and, as my Lord had promised, I had kept his peace in my heart.

As I set the jam pots on the kitchen table whilst waiting for the bubbling mass in the big brass cauldron to cool down I was singing softly to myself, my whole being soaked in that peace. Suddenly I became aware of another voice joining mine from upstairs, a voice which was certainly not singing, rather the reverse, and was growing louder and more insistent every minute.

Going into our six year old son's room I found him standing on a chair, hanging half out of the window: his body was twisted at a peculiar upside-down angle, and his angry red face turned towards the cloudless blue sky.

'Darling,' I said faintly, walking gingerly on tiptoe toward him, fearful that any abrupt noise or movement from me might startle him and topple him out of the window on to the paved courtyard below, 'just what are you doing?'

'I'm talking to God,' Yves replied as, with a swift movement, I grabbed him round the waist.

'Do you *have* to do it quite so loudly,' I gasped, relief almost taking my breath away. 'I'm sure he can hear you.'

'Well, if he can,' my son flung back at me, 'why doesn't he answer?'

I didn't know what to say. His perilous position had terrified me and numbed my brain, catching me completely off my guard.

'Perhaps he's too busy at the moment,' I at last feebly ventured, still breathing rapidly even as the fear for my child's safety gradually receded.

'What's he doing?' Yves shot out, a glimmer of interest in his china-blue eyes.

He had half turned round from his suicidal stance, but my grip on his waist made further movement impossible.

I took a deep breath, not only feeling shaky but also lost and helpless.

'Running the world,' I blurted out, and immediately, with a rush of remorse, realised what I'd said. Even in my unnerved state how *could* I have put the idea into Yves' head that his heavenly Father, who at that time was so real to him, was too busy to answer when he called.

'Well,' Yves went on belligerently, twisting backwards again and staring at the sky from his upside-down perch, preparing to fire yet another volley, 'why doesn't he stop running the world and listen to me when I talk to him?'

I gently untwisted my little son and lifted him off the chair, flopping down amongst the assortment of teddies on his bed with relief at having finally extricated him from danger.

'Darling,' I said gently, drawing him to me, 'I said a stupid thing. Of *course* God can hear you at any time and in any place; he's NEVER too busy to listen when we call.'

I hugged him close and kissed the tip of his silver-blond head.

'And you don't have to fill your lungs to bursting point and let the whole neighbourhood know what you're doing either,' I smiled.

Yves looked up at me and grinned and I realised how near I had come to showing to my little boy a God who was enclosed by our human limitations, a Saviour who had to fit into our time-run existence.

I stood up and held out my hand to him.

'I've just finished making jam from those blackberries we picked yesterday. Would you like to stick the labels on the jars for me?'

His eyes shone with excitement as he ran down the stairs before me into the kitchen. And it was whilst we were working happily together with the fruits of God's harvest that I was able to talk to him about his heavenly Father and explain that God is not limited by time as we are; that he is always there, always ready to listen when we call and that none are more precious to him than his little children.

'Don't you remember learning in Sunday School about how the disciples tried to turn the children away because they thought they would tire Jesus,' I asked.

Yves nodded.

'But what did Jesus do?' I went on. 'Didn't he say to them: "let the little children come to me and do not hinder them, for the kingdom of heaven belongs to such as these."'

He nodded again, licking his sticky fingers.

'You are very important to Jesus, darling,' I said, tipping his chin and looking into those soft blue eyes, 'never forget that.'

Yves looked back at me, wistfully.

'I wish I could have been alive in Jesus's day,' he said softly, 'then I could have sat at his feet too like those children did, and listened to his stories.'

He paused thoughtfully.

'I'd like to have been the little boy with the loaves and the fishes,' he ended simply.

My eyes clouded with tears of pure joy and I hugged him close. His blond hair was sticky and streaked with warm blackberry jam, where he'd twisted the tuft at the back of his head, a gesture he always made when he was tired or thoughtful.

'But you can still listen to him,' I murmured into the warm soft mass. 'Praying is only talking to Jesus and if, when you say your prayers at night, you stop for a moment to listen, Jesus will talk to you and answer your questions and guide you, not only now but every day of your life.'

I paused and looked down at him as he continued to twist the tuft of hair slowly round and round.

'That's what's so wonderful,' I went on. 'Although we can't see him, Jesus is alive and with us all the time; and we only have to call his name and he hears us.'

Yves looked up at me, his eyes still thoughtful.

'And don't forget,' I ended hugging him to me once again, 'Jesus was once a little boy too. You can tell him all your problems because he's been through them. He knows what it is to be young, and he understands.'

As if a light had suddenly dawned, Yves drew away from me and smiled. Then he turned and, running through the open door into the garden, jumped on to the swing.

Looking out of the window at his happy face and seeing his sturdy young legs energetically propelling him higher and higher, my heart swelled and almost burst with love and pride. I realised once again what a wonderful privilege I had, as a mother, to mould this soft clay, this sensitive impressionable little mind, to be able to open my child's eyes to the reality of Jesus in his daily life as his friend and Saviour. To be able to show him that Jesus wasn't just for the little boys in Israel who flocked to hear him on the shores of Lake Galilee nearly two thousand years ago, but that he is alive and here with us now, and all he has to do is call his name and ask him to guide him every step of the way.

How thankful I was that autumn day that God had given me this opportunity to talk to Yves about his Saviour: the Saviour who had said when the people flocked to hear him: 'Anyone who will not receive the kingdom of God like a little child will never enter it.'

As I sat there gazing dreamily through the window the gate

was suddenly thrown open and I heard a thud as Bee's satchel shot into the hall. Hearing her, Yves squealed with delight and, dragging his feet on the ground to stop the swing, rushed into the house after her. They both flung into the kitchen at the same time and, at the sight of the hot jam steaming in the jars, Bee's brown eyes widened.

As the two of them ran happily back into the garden, each with a thick wedge of bread and jam in their hand, and jumped together on to the swing, it gave me a comfortable feeling of security and belonging to see this family tie which had begun with my grandmother's deep attachment to her young brother Cecil, woven its way through the next two generations and was now repeating itself in Yves and Bee. And, seeing this fine thread running through our relationships gave, for me, a structure and meaning to our earthly existence, strengthening Jesus's teaching on the blessedness of family life.

Chapter 13

W FOR ICE-CREAM

Having been an only child for over four years I think I understood more fully the privilege Yves and Bee had of belonging to a 'famille nombreuse', or numerous family as French law calls any family of three children or more.

I had continually pestered my parents for a 'baby' but had received only vague assurances that one might eventually be forthcoming. When, exasperated by all this procrastination, I had enquired about a baby's origins and asked bluntly where they could be procured the answer I received was: 'Jesus brings them in the night.'

And there the matter, and any further discussion, had ended.

I suppose it was a better explanation than the cabbage patch one but it didn't satisfy me, as I could not understand why if Jesus went around distributing babies to families indiscriminately in the night we couldn't not only order one immediately (I had decided to call ours Joan regardless of sex), but also state the colour and the sex we preferred.

I had a black doll which I loved dearly and insisted on taking everywhere long after it should have been consigned to the rubbish heap. I lost it once and was inconsolable until my mother went to great lengths to get it back, finally tracking it down to a bonfire pile where it was perched next to the Guy, all ready to go up in flames on 5 November.

I am sure that the children who had found my doll, in a

park dustbin where it had been dumped after I had forgotten it on a bench, would willingly have handed the decrepit object back to my mother for nothing. They were apparently staggered that anyone would actually pay to retrieve such a wreck, but the doll represented something important to me. It was called Nanina after a nanny I had had when I was very small whom I had loved dearly, and without my substitute Nanina I was inconsolable. Loving this inanimate object as I did I would have opted for a baby of the same colour had I been given the choice.

Just before my brother was born I was sent to stay with Great-Aunt Jessica, and when the telegram announcing his arrival was delivered she opened the buff envelope and, bending down, said to me: 'You've got a baby brother with black curly hair.'

I promptly rushed to the maid who was scrubbing the steps leading to the house and announced excitedly: 'Millie, I've got a black baby brother with curly hair!'

The door to the jungle happened to be open and Uncle Freddie's vast form appeared in the aperture, shaking with uncontrollable laughter at my incongruous statement.

As he shared this choice titbit of news with Percy, who was perched on his shoulder, the monkey added his shrieks and excited chatter to Uncle Freddie's bellows. Seeing me standing there, bewildered by all this high-pitched, incomprehensible amusement and utterly defenceless, the wretched monkey took a flying leap and landed in my hair.

I had always been afraid of this smelly, hairy animal with the large pink paws and ugly face, maybe subconsciously expecting him to rub noses like his master, so I added my shrieks to the general din.

The uproar, which must have been horrific, brought the usually dignified Aunt Jessica running into the hall. Geraldine, who was also staying, appeared just behind her and burst into helpless giggles when she saw my frantic struggles with Percy. But the monkey, seeing Aunt Jessica appear on the scene, jumped from my hair back to Uncle Freddie's shoulder then, stretching up his long skinny arms, swung on to the top of the door frame and scrambled to safety round the picture rail in the jungle, dislodging in the process an impressive picture of Uncle Freddie wearing jungle kit and a topee standing with one foot triumphantly posed on the back of a, presumably dead, lion.

Percy finally dropped to safety on to the arm of his master's old leather armchair and, grabbing a pipe from the collection on the mantelpiece, calmly set about filling it before placing it in the side of his mouth and glaring belligerently over the top of the bowl.

Uncle Freddie, sensing danger in the angry glint in his wife's eyes as she bent to comfort me, closed the door of the jungle on the combined shrieks of Percy and Egbert, who had now entered into an animated conversation, and went to join his so-called dumb companions.

As the general din in the hall gradually died down that day of my brother's arrival in the world, a loud cry of 'Wall's... ice-creeeeeeeeeam-ah' was heard in the road outside and Aunt Jessica obviously concluded that this diversion would banish, quicker than anything else, my hiccoughing sobs. She was absolutely right!

It was just after breakfast and normally we were not allowed to eat between meals but this special August morning in 1930, as a kind of consolation prize, Aunt Jessica sent Geraldine and me to buy ice-cream.

In those days a man wearing a white cap and apron with a large W printed on each, pedalled a refrigerated trunk at intervals round the streets. Some people who lived near the road had large cardboard W's which they placed in their front window when they wanted 'Mr Wall's' to call. I was terribly envious of them, as my passion for this ice-cream pedlar knew no limits and to me the summit of joy would have been to receive this personal attention from my hero.

Looking back, I realise that had I been born forty years

later I would almost certainly have been despatched to a psychiatrist's couch at an early age or, at least, for remedial classes for dyslexia, because it was years before I could be made to understand when reciting my alphabet that W did *not* stand for ice-cream.

Geraldine ran through the garden, dragging me behind her, terrified that Mr Wall's would have pedalled away before we got to him. But it was a hot morning and several people were still standing waiting to be served when we arrived, breathless, on the scene.

In those days it was all 'made to measure', not pre-packed, and one could either buy a cornet or a sandwich, vanilla ice cream tucked between two wafer biscuits, which was slightly more expensive: I think they cost a penny halfpenny instead of the penny we paid for a cornet. Grownups usually had 'sandwiches' as they were more easily eaten in a dignified fashion, but we children loved licking the cornets and, when no one was looking, biting off the narrow tip and noisily sucking the melting ice-cream through the length of the cone.

As the cornets were 'handfilled' it was impossible to make them absolutely identical and this particular morning my eagle eyes noticed that one had definitely more ice-cream in it than the other. As we re-entered the garden – in those days we were never allowed to eat in the street – Geraldine handed me what I thought was the smaller one of the two cornets, which caused another commotion.

The patience Great-Aunt Jessica must have had, and she was no longer young! I remember bursting angrily into the morning room (nobody has a morning room any more, or if they do they call it something else) where she was sitting at her writing desk.

'Aunt Jessica,' I bellowed, 'Geraldine's a GREEDY PIG! She took the biggest ice-cream and *I* wanted it.'

I can't remember my Great-Aunt's reaction but I am sure that she quietly put down her pen, soothed the situation and made things right.

Oddly enough, it had never occurred to me to take my grievance to my grandmother for arbitration. She was still in bed lingering over her breakfast tray, seemingly completely unperturbed by the news of the arrival of her second grandson, her younger daughter, my Aunt Dodo, having presented her with my cousin, Tom, the year before.

It's strange how some events in one's life stand out so clearly, even after more than fifty years, whereas there are other vast expanses of my childhood which hold no particular memories at all.

That day in August 1930 when I stopped being an only child and acquired the longed-for baby is stamped indelibly in my mind. It is even stamped more permanently in an old photograph album of my mother's, showing a sepia portrait of Geraldine and me taken in Great-Aunt Jessica's drawing room later that morning.

Geraldine's older brother, Robin, who had stopped over on his way home from a climbing holiday in Wales, had taken it with some old photographic equipment of Uncle Freddie's which he had found whilst rummaging in the attic. Aunt Jessica lived in Kent, which wasn't exactly on Robin's way home to North Yorkshire, rather *out* of his way, but her house had become a clearing station, a kind of Clapham Junction for all the nieces and nephews and their offspring, who were always turning up unannounced or rendezvousing with each other there, almost as if it were a hotel foyer.

When the photograph was taken I think I must still have been stinging under the impact of Geraldine's appalling greed, because my face is as black as a thundercloud, or perhaps it was just the unexpected flash from the old-fashioned camera and the shock of seeing Robin dive under a black cloth draped over the tripod and then seeing his hand holding the flash appear from nowhere and hearing his muffled voice shout: 'Watch the birdie!'

Whatever the reason, I sat there clutching Nanina with Geraldine smiling beside me – she had after all won the battle

– Michael John her one-eyed, balding teddy bear hanging limply over her arm.

Looking back to the birth of my brother I realise now that I knew absolutely nothing about the miracle which was at work in my mother's body. Pregnancy and birth were never discussed with, or even in front of, children, though I think that had my mother had her way she would have been more open with me and involved me more. But in those days custom died hard and such a thing was unthinkable.

How much more sensible young mothers are today to tell the truth to a child at whatever age it starts asking questions, to let him or her feel the baby's pre-natal movements and watch the mother's body gradually expanding to house the little brother or sister. Even the smallest children understand.

I must have been in my early teens when I finally learned how nature works and it was a shock; it would have been so much easier had my questions been answered truthfully right from the beginning. And it would have saved at least one embarrassing situation! Just before the war we were once again at Great-Aunt Jessica's when Sybil's brother arrived with his young wife, who was expecting their first baby. On seeing her I burst out:

'Imogen, you *have* got fat!'

Nowadays everyone would have laughed, but in the thirties it caused acute embarrassment all round and I was quickly shushed out of the room.

Mercifully with Bee there was no pretence. She was IN right from the start and allowed to watch and feel her two little brothers' pre-natal antics. She even insisted that Yves kicked her out of bed one morning not long before he was born when she had crept in beside me for a cuddle.

At five she had not started asking too many technical questions, though she had frequently dropped heavy hints about being the 'littlest' and followed them up with pleas for a baby. But one evening when she was thrashing about in her bubble bath her pleas for an addition to the family took on dramatic proportions. I knew there was something wrong as Bee, like Christopher after her, was an easy, placid sweet-natured child, but that evening her heart-shaped face was clouded with rage.

'Why can't *I* have a baby like everybody else,' she suddenly stormed, hurtling her unprotesting rubber duck to the far end of the bath.

I must say I hadn't noticed everybody else producing babies, but it was obviously something which was bothering her and, although I wasn't a committed Christian at the time, I took the children to church and had taught them to say their prayers at night. In a vague way I think I may have believed that prayers could possibly be answered, though without any really strong conviction that they would be. But maybe the Holy Spirit was even then beginning to work in my heart for I heard myself saying:

'If you want a little brother or sister that badly, why don't you ask Jesus for one?'

Bee climbed out of the bath in a better mood after hearing my suggestion and, kneeling down beside her bed as usual, said her prayers, adding a special request for the longed for baby.

It happened to be a Saturday and I remember falling into bed exhausted. It was early spring and we had been out on a family picnic all day and the unexpected sunshine had made me sleepy. As I sank into my pillow I was luxuriating in the thought that there was no need to put on the alarm, church wasn't until ten-thirty but long before we needed to be up our 'human' alarms would have awakened us.

But it seemed that I had only just turned over and savoured this glorious promise when I was startled from sleep by an angry little figure shaking me furiously. It must have been all of 5 a.m. Struggling up from the depths of oblivion and focusing with difficulty in the half light, I saw Bee standing there in her short pink nightie, a well-loved teddy bear clutched in her arms and her brown eyes blazing with anger.

'Whatever's the matter?' I slurred, still half asleep.

Bee stamped her bare foot.

'It didn't *come*,' she hissed.

'What didn't?' I mumbled drowsily.

'The baby,' she spat back. 'The baby we asked Jesus for last night. I put my pillow and my dolly's best blanket and my new teddy all ready for it by the side of my bed and . . .'

By now her anger was giving way to tears.

'It didn't *come*!'

And she crumbled in a sobbing heap on the floor.

I got out of bed and knelt beside her, taking the small, shaking body in my arms! But I really did not know what to say, I had never imagined that she would take the prayer literally and expect instant delivery. For me, it had merely been a means of diffusing her anger: yet Jesus told us to pray and that anything we ask in his name which is in line with his Father's will, and I think that is the secret, will be granted to us.

He means us to take him seriously, as children take their earthly fathers seriously. I know that now and it was in line with God's will that Bee should have her baby, but not immediately. Yves only arrived the following year and, as I later explained to him on that golden autumn afternoon, God ALWAYS hears our prayers, but he doesn't always answer them immediately. And sometimes the answer is no . . . or wait.

But that early spring morning I had no real words of comfort for Bee so I just picked the sad little bundle up in my arms and took her back to her room, where the pathetic sight of the improvised cot awaiting the expected baby was there, empty, on the floor beside her own bed. And all I could do was tuck her in and sit by her side and soothe her till she fell back to sleep.

Like all children, Bee quickly forgot her disappointment, but when she knew that Yves was on the way she decided he would be a little sister and prepared for one, even deciding on the name, as I had done all those years before.

She was staying with my parents in Essex when the news was telephoned through that 'Caroline', the expected baby sister, had turned out to be a baby brother, and had apparently cried: 'I don't WANT another brother, put him in the dustbin,' and rushed sobbing into her bedroom, and refused to come out. But once again her disappointment was shortlived and when she arrived home the day after I returned from hospital with the precious bundle I will never forget the look on her face as she raced in front of me up the stairs into the nursery.

She peered into the cot and then turned to me, her dark eyes shining, her face radiant and whispered; 'Don't let's put him in the dustbin after all. We'll keep him till he's two and then see.'

I remember laughing and ruffling her hair before we walked back down the stairs, our arms round each other.

By the time he was two they were firm friends and any thought of disposing of this intruder had been banished.

When I was expecting Christopher three years later, although Bee still hoped for the baby sister, she didn't go to such lengths to prepare for one and when Jacques rang from the hospital early that November morning it was Olivier who took the call.

Running up the stairs he excitedly banged on his little sister's bedroom door shouting: 'It's a baby brother!'

'What?' Bee had answered sleepily.

'A *baby brother*,' Olivier had repeated, opening the door to see her reaction.

She had apparently opened one eye, said, 'Oh blow' and turned over and gone back to sleep!

At least it was less dramatic than the first time!

Chapter 14

THE BABY SITTER

But it was after Christopher arrived that we decided we really ought to have some kind of built-in baby sitter, not only for the times when Jacques and I were out, but also so that I could hear the baby's cries above the racket the other four perpetually seemed to make.

I was extremely tired at the time and we did not go out a great deal but on the evenings when we did, or even when we were all in the house, the mother hen in me wanted to be sure I could hear the baby's least whimper.

'Hear him if he changes his mind,' Jacques used to tease.

The day the baby alarm, or 'the thing' as it became known, was installed happened to be one of those rare occasions when we were going out. We knew we wouldn't be late so, before leaving, we explained to Olivier and Hervé just how the system worked and, as an added precaution 'just in case' her brothers weren't around, we gave a brief rundown to Bee, who was very busy designing a pair of spectacles for a short-sighted horse and didn't show much interest.

We then left home satisfied that Christopher's mere breathing could be heard like an erupting volcano all over the house.

'Everything been all right?' I ventured when we returned, putting down my handbag and gloves and walking into the drawing room.

'Mmmm,' came anonymously from the depths of an

armchair where Bee's bosom friend had her nose in a book.

'Did Christopher cry?' I pursued further, slightly irritated at their lack of enthusiasm for this dazzling new piece of electrical equipment which had come into their lives.

'Oh yes, three times,' said Bee without removing her face from the Jew's harp she had now turned her energies to, the short-sighted horse obviously having been catered for.

'What was the matter with him?' I queried anxiously.

'*I* don't know,' she gasped, coming up for a brief gulp of air. Her friend didn't even bother to raise her eyes.

I was beginning to lose patience.

'But didn't you go upstairs and find out?' I rasped.

'Of course not,' Bee answered scathingly.

My lips tightened.

'What *did* you do then?'

'Oh,' gasped Bee coming up for air yet again, 'we went up to that thing on the wall and yelled SHUT UP.'

I just stood and gaped at her, unable to believe my ears.

'And did he?' I finally managed to get out.

'You bet,' she replied and returned to her twanging.

Negotiating the stairs in about three jumps I skidded along the landing to the baby's room – there he lay in his cot, warm and rosy-cheeked, sleeping peacefully.

I turned a bewildered look at Jacques who had followed me at a more leisurely pace.

'Do *you* think I fuss too much?' I queried pitifully.

'No,' he soothed, looking down fondly at the sleeping baby, 'but Bee's unusual method does seem to have done the trick.'

He put his arm round my shoulders as we turned away.

'The Bible says,' he remarked softly, 'he shall give his angels charge over thee.'

I looked up at him questioningly as we went downstairs to explain to Bee that the whole idea of the listening device was so that she could go and find out *why* her baby brother was crying, not so that she could yell at him to shut up.

'I think we've seen this promise in action tonight,' my

husband said quietly.

I didn't answer but, for the moment, my constant fears for the baby were stilled. God really had sent his angels to keep charge of our precious child, in spite of his big sister's apparent neglect.

I don't think Jacques was consciously witnessing to me when he said those words: I was pretty neurotic at the time and still only a churchgoer and not a committed Christian like my husband. But as I look back I feel that perhaps there was more than comfort in the passage which he quoted, there was a small seed which fell on the fertile soil of my anxious heart and, little by little, helped me to understand my husband's total trust in Jesus, his security and his peace in the midst of the storms which, when Christopher was a baby, began to remorselessly rock the little barque of our family life. I sometimes wonder how he survived those traumatic two years following Christopher's birth, with all the calls on his time, his energy, his emotions.

I know now that it was because of his daily walk with Jesus.

Chapter 15

SURRENDER

Later that evening when we were sitting together, the house at last quiet, I put down the book I was reading and looked across at my husband.

'How do you do it?' I asked.

Jacques lowered the report he was reading.

'Do what?' he enquired.

'Oh, I don't know,' I went on, 'you always seem to see the bright side of everything, never be afraid or anxious, always to have peace.'

He laid his pen on the table in front of him and, reaching into his pocket, took out a small Bible.

'It's all in here,' he said, tapping the cover, and opening it, he read out the first verse of Psalm 27.

'The Lord is my light and my salvation; whom shall I fear? The Lord is the stronghold of my life, of whom shall I be afraid?'

He looked up. 'Do you want me to go on?' he enquired.

I nodded and he read on to the end of verse eight:

'When the evil men advance against me to devour my flesh, when my enemies and foes attack me they stumble and fall. Though an army besiege me, my heart will not fear: though war break out against me, even then will I be confident. One thing I ask of the Lord, that is what I seek: that I may dwell in the house of the Lord all the days of my life, to gaze upon the beauty of the Lord and to seek him in his temple. For in the day of trouble he will keep me safe in his dwelling; he will hide me in the shelter of his tabernacle and set me high upon a rock. Then my head will be exalted above the enemies who surround me; at his tabernacle will I sacrifice with shouts of joy; I will sing, and make music to the Lord. Hear my voice when I call, be merciful to me and answer me. My heart says of you "seek his face". Your face, Lord, I will seek.'

Then he closed the book and put it back in his pocket.

'The Bible also assures us that God will keep in perfect peace those whose minds are stayed on him,' he smiled.

'But aren't you afraid of anything?' I enquired, slightly exasperated at his calmness.

'Such as?' he queried.

'Well, dying...'

'It's the only thing in life we can be sure of,' my husband replied laconically.

'I know,' I answered, irritated, 'but it's frightening all the same. No one really knows what happens.'

'Don't they?' Jacques said quietly and looked straight at me. 'My Bible says that when I die my heavenly Father will be waiting for me.'

And, leaning forward, he took up his pen and turned back to his report.

I picked up my book and tried to read but my mind kept churning over what Jacques had said.

In a way I believed him, or at least I wanted to believe him, but I couldn't be sure. As if we must be sure of everything in life. And yet I know now that we can be sure, can have the answer to that one question which seems to trouble so many people: what happens after death? Almost as if I needed confirmation from another source, not long afterwards I heard a story which brought to life what Jacques had said that evening.

Jane was an only child, just eight years old when her mother died and, shortly afterwards, her father was sent to work for a year on an oil exploration project in Saudi Arabia. As it was not possible for him to take his little daughter with him she was left behind with her maternal grandparents but, the first school holidays after his departure, he sent for her to join him.

As she walked up the steps to the aeroplane Jane held on confidently to the hostess's hand, her doll clutched tightly to her. Before disappearing inside, she turned and waved happily to her grandparents, who were leaning anxiously over the airport terrace watching the tiny speck in the checked cotton frock and the bright school blazer.

She had a long tedious journey ahead of her and at times during the flight she was restless and bored: at other times the sheer monotony of the endless hours in space and the rhythm of the aircraft lulled her to sleep.

As the plane circled and prepared to land the hostess, who was helping Jane to fasten her seat belt, said sympathetically, 'It's been a long tiring journey for you. I expect you're glad we've almost arrived.'

'Yes,' Jane smiled, 'it was, but Grannie told me it would be.'

Then, with shining eyes, she looked up at the hostess and said, 'But it's been worth it because I know that my father will be waiting for me when I get there.'

That story cemented for me Jacques' words and explained more clearly his peace and his certainty of salvation.

At that particular time my husband's life was cramped and tiring, full of tedious stops and detours, and he must sometimes have asked himself where it was leading. But in spite of all the insurmountable problems which crushed in on Jacques during those years in the mid-sixties when he not only had a responsible job and a heavy workload, but five children and a depressed, neurotic wife to cope with, he knew for certain where he was going.

He knew in which direction his life was heading, but more

importantly he knew who was guiding it. And just as Jane had the promise that her earthly father would be there to meet her when she arrived at the end of her long journey, so Jacques had the same promise from his heavenly Father. Like Yves, as we burst out of the dark tunnel into the dazzling sunlight, Jacques could confidently say:

'*Now* I understand about eternity.'

And we begin to understand and to get a glimpse of eternity when we believe and accept for ourselves those precious words of Jesus: 'Whoever believes in me shall not perish but have eternal life.'

Salvation is a gift, God's gift to his children. It cannot be inherited, or deserved or even earned, for the Bible tells us: 'It is by grace you have been saved, through faith and this not from yourselves, it is the gift of God, *not by works*, so that no one can boast.'

And those who have accepted this precious gift, have this blessed assurance of eternal life with him.

Only a few days ago someone said to me; 'What's the point of eternal life?'

He was a young man and I understood what he meant, as I had felt the same way at his age.

When we are twenty with our life before us, as he was, we have so many plans, so many dreams and the world is there at our feet for us to discover and enjoy. And if one hasn't already met Jesus and accepted him as Saviour, it is difficult to imagine that we really need him at all. I know it was for me and it still is for many.

I burst out of my teens as the war ended and we all believed that from then onwards life would be beautiful; we had fought the war to end all wars, there was simply to be the brotherhood of men from that day forth and the world could not but be a better place.

Or so we thought.

Had anyone come to me in 1945 and presented Jesus's plan for salvation I very much doubt whether I would have accepted it. Oh, like everyone else, I had cried out to God many times during those terrible six years in fear and pain, in utter helplessness because there had been no one else to turn to. But once it was over then, together with thousands of other eager, idealistic young people we had pledged to work out the beautiful future for ourselves, to make a land fit for heroes.

It took over twenty years of striving to make it on my own before I capitulated and admitted that 'without me you can do nothing'. And when Jesus said 'nothing' he meant nothing: he didn't mean you can't do very much, but purely and simply nothing.

It's hard to capitulate, to totally surrender and give over everything, be like a helpless babe in his hands, especially when one is young and not long released from the restrictions of adolescence. For me the hardest part was to recognise that a great part of myself was made up of pride, and until I came face to face with that eroding aspect of my life I was not able to understand the futility of trying to make it on my own.

Giving up my life to Jesus was one thing, but surrendering my pride was another ... until I actually did it, and then I wondered why on earth I hadn't done it years before!

I had not realised until then that God never forces anything, and especially not the surrender of ourselves and our will. He waits until we yield them up to him. And when that is done, all is done and we are free to be ourselves as he always wanted us to be. The great crisis is over, there is no longer a dichotomy in our hands. And no other crisis can ever affect us so deeply.

As I looked across at my young friend I saw the connection between his question 'what is the point of eternal life?' and the reply Pilate made to Jesus when our Lord told him: 'I came into the world to testify to the truth.' And Pilate had replied; 'What is truth?'

I felt that this young man was asking the very same question and, in a way, he was not unlike Pilate.

When Jesus was brought to him for trial, Pilate half believed his claims and wanted to release him, finding no fault in him: he had even been afraid of Jesus's calm insistence that he was indeed a king and his serenity in the face of his trial and almost certain conviction. But the crowd waiting outside was out for blood, Jesus's blood. They were not prepared to accept an acquittal and, allowing himself to be swayed by the mob and by popular opinion, Pilate had given in and handed Jesus over to be crucified.

Perhaps this young man half believed too.

But it's too easy to be swayed by the mob, by popular opinion, by what other people say and think. And, nowadays, with God thrown out of the schools and a bewildering clutter of other beliefs and deities put in his place, it is not easy for young people to find the truth, unless they are taught it in their own homes. And, even then, when they go out in the world, peer pressure can often be so strong that unless the foundations of their faith are indeed built on rock they can very easily be swayed or crumble.

The only thing I could do in answer to this young man's question was to open my pocket New Testament and read to him Jesus's words: 'Now this is eternal life, to know you, the only true God and Jesus Christ whom you have sent.'

And I added: 'Only eternal life can make sense of the hopeless mess of our life down here and the injustices we see round us every day, why one is born poor and one rich, why one is whole and another handicapped, and for which there is no human explanation.'

He made no comment and I don't know whether my words touched him or not. Perhaps he was too young to think of life as a hopeless mess or even see its injustices. Perhaps he has not yet experienced sorrow or loss. I don't know. Maybe those words will only speak to him when he comes face to face with his own mortality. He merely smiled at me and said: 'I suppose I shall understand one day. I must say I've been thinking about it.'

How many people spend all their lives thinking about eternal life without ever getting any further, without realising that they can understand now.

It is not study or deep intellectual thinking which brings about that sudden flash of truth, but obedience to Jesus's call to come to him. God cannot speak to us until we do, until we answer the call of his Spirit to our spirit. But once we do our prayer life becomes vital and alive and when we call we hear his answer, not always in actual words but often through events or circumstances or unexpected happenings in our lives.

Sometimes even through our children!

Chapter 16

THE RAINBOW

It was one rainy summer day which had left me without resources. I had promised to take Yves and Christopher on an outing to the Jardin d'Acclimatation, a zoo combined with roundabouts and swings situated in the Bois de Boulogne, the beautiful woods which border the western periphery of Paris. However, in pouring rain it would have been a disaster and I had to think of something else to take its place.

Ideas for keeping two boys happy and occupied were running thin when I suddenly remembered a jigsaw puzzle which they had received for Christmas a few years earlier and, neither of them being madly enthusiastic about anything which required their sitting still for more than three minutes flat, it had never even been opened.

I decided that now was the time!

After showing them the picture of a large map of the world I broke it up and told them to put it together again and, shutting the door behind me, heard them eagerly attacking this new challenge. Sighing with relief I settled back with a book, convinced that the task would occupy them for the rest of the afternoon, but in no time at all the door opened and they triumphantly appeared carrying the completed puzzle on the tray between them.

I looked up in amazement.

'Did Bee come and help you?' I enquired.

Their elder sister was quite clever with puzzles but, as far as

I remembered, she was seated happily on the floor of her room listening to records with her current bosom friend.

'No,' Yves announced triumphantly, 'we did it all by ourselves.'

'That's wonderful,' I said none too enthusiastically, seeing my peace fade and racking my brain for further ideas to keep them happy for the rest of the afternoon.

'But how did you do it so quickly?' I enquired, intrigued. Christopher, at seven, had probably never seen a map of the world and Yves at ten couldn't be all that familiar with its intricacies. 'A map isn't an easy puzzle to fit together.'

'Oh,' Yves said, 'we didn't do the map.'

I stared at him, frowning: his words didn't make sense.

'What *did* you do then?'

'The other side,' Christopher piped up. 'When you brought the puzzle down Yves saw on the box that there was a man on the other side so we turned all the bits over and put the man together.'

I was beginning to understand: on the other side of the map of the world was a close-up of the face of a famous astronaut.

'Yes,' Yves broke in, 'the world was too hard for us, but we knew what a man looked like, so we put him together and when we'd got him right it was easy, we turned the pieces over and the world came out right.'

'How clever you are,' I murmured, stooping to gather them both in a gigantic hug, the hidden truth behind their triumphant statement slowly dawning on me, but not exactly in the way they had meant it.

As Yves had said, they knew what a man looked like, and when *he* had been put right, the world came right.

And I heard myself murmuring into the softness of their hair Jesus's words: 'I praise you Father, Lord of heaven and earth, because you have hidden these things from the wise and learned and revealed them to little children.'

'What did you say?' Yves enquired, looking up.

'Nothing darling,' I whispered, giving them a final hug.

And, as I did so, I looked out of the window. The rain had stopped and a large multicoloured rainbow splashed across the sky. God's covenant with man. His promise to Noah when after forty days the rain ceased and the waters began to go down and the old wicked world all of whom, except Noah and his family, had rejected God had perished, God swore that he would never again destroy the world by flood.

I looked down at the intact map of the world knowing that, if I turned it over as the boys had done, the astronaut's face would smile up at me from the other side. And I wondered if it were an omen that summer afternoon: the rainbow, God's covenant and promise, and the astronaut looking out on the other side of the world, to other worlds as yet untapped. To worlds which we could not see, did not even know about, but which God had strung across the planet like myriad stars in the sky, which his hands had made. Worlds which, perhaps, without God, men would destroy in some other way, by fire or nuclear holocaust. And in Yves' innocent statement I saw revealed the truth that Jesus taught nearly two thousand years ago: that it is not the world which is wrong, it is the heart of man.

From Bee's room the strains of a popular record floated down the stairs. 'What the world needs is love, love love' crooned the singer and I heard myself saying tightly: 'It's not love that the world needs, but surgery, drastic heart surgery, and when man's heart is put right the world will fall into place.'

Christopher came up beside me, where I was still standing gazing at the rainwashed sky, and slipped his hand in mine.

'It's stopped raining,' he said, 'can we go out?'

I roused myself from my dreaming and squeezed his little hand.

'Yes, let's,' I answered enthusiastically. 'Run and get your football and I'll take you to the park.'

The two boys raced off excitedly and I turned and once again looked down sadly at the tray bearing the map of an intact world.

Chapter 17

I LOST AND FOUND

'What exactly did you promise to bring the children back?' Jacques enquired.

It was the last day of a Christian seminar which we were attending in Switzerland, and we were preparing to go to the afternoon session.

'Well,' I began, 'I did say watches and alarm clocks. They are so much cheaper here.'

'And you've promised EACH of them a watch or an alarm clock?'

'Yes,' I answered defensively, a little puzzled.

Jacques is the most generous person I've ever known and I couldn't understand why he was interrogating me about money. He sensed my surprise and laughed.

'I'm not reproaching you,' he said. 'I just want to put the money aside. We don't have a great deal left I'm afraid. Apart from a few odd coins this is all there is.'

And taking a large bank-note from his wallet he held it up.

'That be enough?' he enquired.

'Oh easily,' I replied, 'more than enough, I hope.'

Jacques slipped it back into his wallet as we left our room.

At the close of the meeting an unexpected announcement was made: there was to be a special collection taken that evening at the close of the seminar and we were all asked to pray about it beforehand and give according to how God led us.

I looked at Jacques as we rose to leave the convention hall, for the offering had come as a complete surprise.

'How much money do we have left?' I whispered.

'One last bank-note,' replied my husband serenely.

'The one you put aside to buy the children's presents?' I queried.

'The very one,' he answered.

My heart sank.

'Haven't you got *any* other money?' I asked helplessly.

'Why should I have?' Jacques smiled. 'Tomorrow evening we'll be in Paris; no point in taking a whole lot of Swiss francs home with us. I told you I'd budget what we have to cover our stay here, and that's what I've done. There's just those few odd coins left for tips.'

I suddenly felt a surge of anger and frustration well up in me.

'Oh, *what* a fool I was to lose my wallet with our French francs in,' I burst out, furious with myself all over again.

We had arrived in Interlaken a day early and taken advantage of the opportunity to visit the surrounding beauty spots; and somewhere during that trip I had lost my wallet, in which we had put all our French money for safety.

Jacques smiled and took my arm. 'Getting angry won't bring it back,' he remarked, 'what's done is done.'

My husband has always had a casual attitude towards money which I have never entirely shared.

'I don't suppose there's much hope of it turning up now,' I said miserably. 'There's been no word from the police.'

'Shouldn't think there's the slightest chance,' Jacques answered nonchalantly, looking down at me indulgently.

'Don't WORRY,' he soothed.

'But what shall we do?' I wailed.

'What the last speaker told us to do,' he replied equably, 'pray about it. Come on, the lift doors are about to close.'

Once back in our room Jacques took the precious note out of his wallet and laid it on the table.

'There we are,' he said, 'now let's ask the Lord what he wants us to do with it.'

'Father,' he said, 'we've been taken by surprise; we didn't expect this collection and the children have been promised presents. But it's your money, Lord, you gave it to us and we want to use it whatever way you tell us to.'

And we remained kneeling in silence. After a few minutes Jacques raised his head.

'I have a distinct feeling that the Lord wants us to give that note to the collection this evening,' he said quietly.

I nodded.

'I do too,' I replied.

'Well then, that's settled,' my husband smiled.

'But Jacques,' I said anxiously, 'what are we going to tell the children?'

'The truth, of course,' he answered.

I bit my lip.

'Do you think they'll be terribly disappointed?' I went on.

'Perhaps,' he replied pensively, 'I don't know. Anyway, let's see what happens, after all you can hardly call them deprived, they can very well live without Swiss watches for a few more years.'

'Yes, I suppose you're right,' I said, relieved. 'But we did promise.'

'*You* did, you mean,' he laughed.

'Oh all right, I did,' I answered, on the defensive. 'But a promise IS a promise – especially to children.'

'Then God will honour it,' my husband replied quietly. 'And now stop worrying and come and have dinner.'

The closing speaker was very moving and when he ended and the seminar was finally over the plate was passed around and I saw our last precious bank-note disappear: but I felt completely at peace about our decision. As the music stopped and chairs began to scrape across the polished floor, as people started moving away, a pretty young American girl who had been sitting in front of us turned round and touched

Jacques' arm. We had met her during the meetings but only casually and she wasn't one of those with whom we had formed a friendship.

Jacques smiled at her and, as he did so, she pressed something into his hand.

'The Lord told me to give you this,' she said.

Absolutely dumbfounded, my husband looked down to see a wad of Swiss bank-notes.

'But...' he began.

'I know what you're going to say,' she said quickly, 'but please don't. It's hard for you to accept it, I know, but it's even harder for me to give it to you. You could be my father and I've never done such a thing before.'

For a moment Jacques was speechless.

'Are you sure you haven't made a mistake?' he said gently.

There were people from Eastern Europe and the Third World at the meeting who had nothing; it would have made sense had she given the money to them.

'No mistake,' she replied firmly. 'The message was very clear that God wanted me to give it to *you*. I just had to.'

Her husband had turned round and now joined in the conversation.

'After we'd put aside the money for the collection,' he explained, 'we really thought we'd spent up, then Debbie found these notes in a zipped pocket of her purse, so we decided to add them to the collection; but we both had a strong feeling that the Lord didn't want us to and we couldn't understand why. We're leaving at six o'clock tomorrow morning and a whole lot of Swiss francs would have been useless to us in the States. Debbie prayed about it all during the closing hymn and had a distinct message from the Lord to turn round and give it to the man sitting directly behind her. So, you see, you have to accept it. We don't know why you need that money, but God does.'

I think all four of us were thunderstruck. But Dave broke the silence with a laugh.

'Let's all go and get some hot chocolate,' he said. 'That's something I'm sure going to miss when we get back to Texas.'

And we went joyfully to the little auberge opposite the conference hall, to start a friendship which has continued by post ever since.

'How much did God lead Debbie to give you?' I asked when we finally got back to our room that night.

Jacques spread out the notes.

'Exactly what he told us to give to the collection,' he replied quietly. I slumped onto the bed in bewilderment.

'I told you God would honour your promise to the children,' Jacques said gently sitting down beside me. 'And you see . . . he has.'

I nodded dumbly unable, for the moment, to speak.

'But you're not going to keep that money are you?' I finally whispered.

'I don't know what to do,' he mused. 'I don't like the idea of doing so, but I can't give it back to them, it would be too hurtful.'

We sat in silence for a moment.

'The Lord obviously led Debbie to give it to you for a reason,' I said at last, 'but I'm sure it wasn't so that the children could have Swiss watches.'

'So am I,' Jacques replied, and we again lapsed into a thoughtful silence.

'I know what we'll do,' my husband said at last. 'God has shown us this evening that he answers prayers in a powerful way, so let's give the money to those Third World delegates or the students from the Bible College so that they can buy tapes or books to take back with them, and trust him to see that the children aren't disappointed.'

'But how?' I wailed.

'I don't know,' Jacques smiled, 'but Jesus does.'

I looked at my husband and smiled slowly, nodding my head in agreement. And that's exactly what we did.

Knowing we would not see Dave and Debbie again before

their early morning start we telephoned and told them what we proposed to do with the gift the Lord had prompted them to give us.

'It's your money,' Dave laughed, 'you do just what you want with it, it'll be OK by us.'

We were just finishing breakfast when the telephone rang. It was a call from the police station.

'The wallet you reported as lost last Wednesday has been handed in, madame.'

I gasped, unable to believe my ears.

'Oh,' I finally managed to get out, 'I'd almost given up hope.'

'It was found in a small sub post office near the Schilthorn,' the smooth voice went on, 'and it has taken time to trace you. But it is now here whenever you wish to call and pick it up.'

I put down the phone in a daze.

'What did I tell you?' Jacques laughed.

'But I can't understand it,' I replied. 'They said it had been found in a small sub post office near the Schilthorn.'

The Schilthorn is a famous Swiss beauty spot and one of the highest Alpine peaks.

'However did it get there?' I frowned, and I thought back over the past week trying to find an explanation.

'Of course,' I exclaimed, after a few moments' silence. 'Don't you remember the first day we were here, the conference didn't start till the evening and we decided to go off and see the Schilthorn. We stopped in a tiny village up in the mountains for lunch and it was then I remembered that it was Margaret's mother's ninetieth birthday the next day and I hadn't sent her a telegram before we left Paris?'

Jacques nodded.

'I mostly remember the problem I had finding you a post office in that isolated place,' he smiled.

I started to giggle and my husband looked up at me enquiringly.

'I was just thinking about that funny old woman who ran it;

she'd never heard of Wales and insisted that Penycraig didn't exist because she couldn't find it in her book.'

Jacques smiled.

'Then the fuss she made saying Brynderwen wasn't an address and she needed a house number and a street name, and it was only when I took out my wallet and showed her that letter I'd received from Margaret just before we left with the address engraved at the top that she grudgingly agreed to send the wire. *That* must have been when I lost the wallet, she got me in such a state.'

We both laughed.

'Only hope the greetings arrived,' I said wryly.

Margaret was my oldest friend and Yves' godmother. I had known her and her husband, Gareth, since we were children and it was her mother who had taught me to do Italian quilting one wartime summer when I had been sent to Wales to escape the bombs. That hot August, Margaret and I had both made ourselves nightdress cases, I a pink one and she a pale blue, sitting stitching in the garden for hour after hour, our ears glued to the wireless set which we had left blaring in the house (no portable transistors in those days) listening to the Forces' Programme churning out recordings of the Glenn Miller band or Vera Lynn throatily crooning 'We'll meet again'.

As these far-off memories came rushing back to my mind, I wondered how many of today's fifteen year olds would be content to spend their school holidays so unspectacularly. In this frantic, time-ridden, pressurised era in which we now live, young people grow up so much more quickly, or is it that we, in our present sophistication, our thirst for instant everything, have hastened the process, cutting short their childhood, that childhood which can be so rich in memories not only for children but for parents too, and turned them into adults before their time?

Margaret's mother had filled my young mind with many happy memories, so I had been upset that winter afternoon in the mountains above Interlaken at the thought that her ninetieth birthday should go by unrecognised by me. She now lived alone in that same house which had once rocked not only to the Forces' Programme's canned music, but to the sound of her daughter and me singing duets and playing the piano together in her dignified drawing room.

As I smiled nostalgically, another less pleasant thought suddenly struck me.

'Do you think the money will still be in it?' I queried, my initial euphoria evaporating at the thought of perhaps only retrieving an empty wallet.

'Don't worry,' Jacques soothed, 'the Swiss are pretty honest, you know.'

I grimaced, pessimistic as usual.

'Where's your faith?' he teased, putting his arm round my shoulders. 'We asked the Lord to find a solution and now that he has you're doubting. Let's go and find out and put you to shame.'

We both laughed and walked out of the hotel in the direction of the police station.

My wallet was intact, even Margaret's letter was still tucked inside it. It just 'so happened' that there was a bank where we were able to change the recovered French francs almost next door to the police station and a watchmaker on the opposite corner who supplied all we needed.

Jacques and I returned home rejoicing in the power of prayer and the reality of a God who is really there.

I had once again reached one of those mountain tops in my Christian walk when Jesus really did as God promised in the last book of the Old Testament 'throw open the floodgates of heaven and pour out so much blessing that you will not have room enough for it.'

Chapter 18

SIX HOURS WHICH CHANGED
THE WORLD

This Swiss interlude had been our first holiday alone, without any children and, after the exhilaration of seeing God so powerfully at work in our lives, when we returned home to find that no major catastrophe had hit the house, no one had been rushed to hospital and everything seemed to be going on very well without me, I suddenly came face to face with my own mortality and realised that my time of 'usefulness', my indispensability as a mother was drawing to its close and I was now middle-aged. That in fact, life was passing me by without my having seen all those youthful post-war dreams come true.

As this thought sank in I understood how poignant it must be for those who do not have the promise of eternity at the end of the tunnel and can only face middle age watching their bodies growing older and becoming less agile, and seeing the years pass by without any hope at the end. And I began to think back to all those friends I had grown up with, all those who, with me, had dreamed our post-war dreams and I wondered how many had, in fact, fulfilled them. Some of them probably did, but perhaps not all that many.

When we are twenty there is so much time. When we reach thirty there is a little less; at forty those early ambitions, though receding, still seem attainable. But by the time the fifties roll along, most of us realise we are not going to win the

London marathon, marry the handsome prince and live happily in a palace ever after, see our name up in lights outside a West End theatre, sing that famous aria to a standing ovation at Covent Garden, or make a name for ourselves at the Old Vic, in parliament, at Wimbledon, in big business or wherever.

Life has crept up on us and other things have taken over, usually far less spectacular than the ones our youthful dreams were coloured with. And sometimes we tend to compare ourselves with famous people of our own age whose dreams, on the surface, have come true and often a feeling of emptiness creeps in – the emptiness which stems from the realisation that life is passing us by and a new generation has taken over with all *their* hopes and dreams.

I sometimes look back and wonder if my own mother felt like that in her fifties and feel sorry for my lack of understanding.

But, I wonder, has life really passed us by?

The night before he died Jesus took a bowl of water and a towel and washed his disciples' feet, a task only the lowliest slave was ever expected to perform in a Middle Eastern household two thousand years ago. And one not many people would relish performing today! Peter, that rough, impetuous, lovable disciple protested loudly at his Lord performing this menial task for him, but Jesus gently pointed out that in order to be great it is necessary to serve others: an idea absolutely contrary to all the thinking of his day – and of our day too!

Jesus said that in many cases those who are first down here on earth will be the last in his kingdom where the humble and meek will be exalted.

I find those words a wonderful comfort and encouragement for us middle-aged mums, who sometimes feel that life has slipped by without our youthful hopes ever being realised and that 'others' have succeeded where we have 'failed'. I occasionally get myself into this pointless rut, usually when I

am tired or have had an overdose of the media telling me, yet
again, to fulfil myself. Then I tend to grind my teeth and
compare myself to Mrs Thatcher, who is my vintage, and
ruminate on what she has achieved.

'How is it she can rush around the world, attend endless
meetings, give press conferences, entertain foreign dignitaries
and always look as if she's just walked out of a bandbox,
never tired and never a hair out of place,' I exploded one
evening, throwing down a glossy magazine showing a large,
smiling picture of the prime minister on the front page.

'She doesn't have to do the shopping and cooking when
she entertains, nor does she look after grandchildren when
their parents want a day off,' Jacques replied laconically
without even raising his eyes from his newspaper. 'And when
she goes flying round the world she doesn't take the airport
bus and queue up at the reception counter to get her luggage
registered or hang around waiting for it when she arrives.'

'All the same, she has ten times more energy than *I* have,' I
sulked. 'It's not fair.'

'Maybe she has,' Jacques agreed, this time looking up
from his newspaper and smiling indulgently, as if at a spoilt
child who was having a tantrum, 'but we're not all the same
and that's all there is to it.'

And, of course, he was right. Mercifully, we are not all the
same. As Jesus said, we are all parts of the same body, with
God as the head, and each part has a different function, not a
more important function, but a different one to perform.

'If we believe in Jesus,' Jacques went on, 'we happily
accept his plan for our lives irrespective of whether it leads us
to be important or insignificant.'

He got up and, crossing to the window, stood looking
across the garden at the shadows which were slowly creeping
across the lawn.

'Has it ever occurred to you,' he said quietly, 'that all the
words ever recorded by Jesus amount to just six hours?'

I frowned, not understanding what he meant.

'But the Bible says that if everything he did and said were recorded all the books in the world couldn't hold them,' I argued.

Jacques swung gently backwards and forwards on his heels, still gazing out at the darkening garden.

'Yes,' he agreed, 'but they *weren't* recorded. Of those which were, we only have six hours' worth of reading.'

He turned and looked at me where I sat on the sofa, lost in thought.

'Jesus didn't have any notes, he didn't have a microphone to reach the crowds, there was no television or satellite to flash him into everyone's living room, there was no radio to broadcast what he said, billboards to announce his coming or newspapers to report his meetings. But, in spite of all that, his words remain twenty centuries later, and his Book is a best-seller which is still changing lives.'

He paused and smiled down at me.

'Makes you think, doesn't it?'

I nodded.

'Makes you realise too how ephemeral earthly fame is.' He paused and stroked his chin reflectively. 'How many other speeches or meetings from AD 30 are still being widely read? Or how many "great names" from that time are even remembered?'

Jacques turned back to gaze at the twilit garden, his hands plunged deep in his pockets.

'Do you remember how disappointed you were in Los Angeles?' he went on. 'You'd been longing to see Hollywood, all that glamour and the screen stars you remembered from before the war?'

I nodded.

'And yet when I took you there you wished you'd never come, it was such a let-down.'

I saw what my husband meant and remembered walking down Hollywood Boulevard and standing in the sunshine outside the famous Chinese Theatre, to study the names of the stars whose hands and feet had been imprinted in cement for posterity.

I knew many of them from my youth in the 30s, the golden age of the silver screen, but I remember thinking that very few of them would be familiar to our children.

'Do you remember what you said?' Jacques enquired.

'Yes,' I smiled. 'I only hoped they were not relying on footprints in cement to give them immortality.'

'*Sic transit gloria mundi*,' Jacques murmured to himself.

Not being a Latin scholar I looked across at my husband enquiringly.

'So vanishes this world's glory,' he smiled as he turned from the window and, crossing the room, took down a large leather-bound encyclopaedia which had been part of his grandfather's library.

It was dated 1900.

'Here,' he said, sitting down beside me, 'this book is full of people who have done outstanding things, famous in their time.'

He paused, and flicked over the pages.

'Famous ninety-odd years ago,' he went on drily. 'Do any of them mean anything to you?'

We peered down the pages together.

I'd hardly heard of any of them and, like the Hollywood idols, the next generation would probably not know even one; and yet, in their day, they had all been 'famous'.

'Remember that chorus you like so much?' Jacques said, closing the book and returning it to the bookcase. 'Turn your eyes upon Jesus, look full in his wonderful face, and the things of earth will grow strangely dim in the light of his glory and grace.'

I glanced down at the glossy magazine I had been reading, all anger and resentment now gone, and I saw what my husband meant.

Chapter 19

ONE OF THE WOMEN I MOST ADMIRED

I don't think anyone epitomised the words of that chorus more for me than Ileana; and as I remember her I realise yet again that the people who influence us most in our Christian walk are not always those who buttonhole us and talk, who hit us on the head with their Bibles, but those whose lives show what they believe. Those who, like Ileana, live their lives as Jesus told us to do, like the lilies of the field, simply, unaffectedly. It is their lives which mould and impress us. I think she is one of the women I have most admired in my life, yet I never knew her in her heyday, when she was 'somebody'.

'I was born with a home, a country and a fortune,' she once told me, 'now I am alone, helpless, stateless and penniless.'

She looked up and smiled.

I could have added: 'You are also ageless, dear Ileana.'

Her deep blue eyes were still bright and twinkling, although the white hair which peeped out from the coloured bandeau she always wore round her head, and the deep lines traced on her cheeks and forehead, showed not only that she had suffered but that the years were beginning to take their toll. I never knew her age until I saw it on her coffin – seventy-nine years – and yet for well over thirty of them she had lived as a cripple in one room, relying on others not only for food but for her very existence.

And yet she was not unhappy; I never saw her anything but content and smiling. She had what most people are searching for today, a serenity which sprang from her deep, enduring faith in the promises of Jesus, and it was that which carried her across life's ocean and enabled her to stay on the crest of each successive wave.

Her room was sparsely furnished, merely the bare necessities, but one didn't even notice it – one only saw Ileana. She had that special 'something', that charisma which so often, like an aura, surrounds those people we meet who are strangely different. In this world yet not of it.

Looking back I think, in a different way, Pierrot had it too, which probably explains why my children liked Ileana and never minded going to see her, although there wasn't much for them to do when they got there. But they had adopted her when they were quite young and called her Tante Ileana, which delighted her as she no longer had any close relatives of her own.

But it had not always been like this.

She was born into a wealthy family in Rumania and, until 1940, Europe had been her playground; but her home was shattered during the last war and her fortune and treasures with it. Since then she had been alone, a refugee, her horizon bounded by the grey roofs of Paris seen through her attic window, and all that remained of her colourful past were a few faded yellow photographs.

'I still have my sister and her children in Rumania,' she once told me, 'but they are now poor and, in any case, I cannot go to see them.'

She paused and added sadly; 'And they would not be able to come to see me.'

She gazed pensively out of the window.

'I haven't seen the purple-green mountains of Transylvania where I spent my happy childhood for over forty years,' she murmured wistfully.

She paused again and seemed far away and I didn't know what to say, but she turned and looked directly at me, **patting my hand.**

'I'm not unhappy,' she smiled. 'I have found the secret of inner peace, the true meaning of life. My faith in God has been honed and sharpened the hard way, through tragedy, through misfortune and through the bitterness of seeing all the material things I once valued, crumble.'

Ileana leant forward and pushed some crumbs across the table and the sparrows which had been twittering on the sill flew in through the open window and began pecking at them.

'You seem so peaceful, Ileana, so contented,' I murmured, as I watched the birds circling above the table before flying back into the sunshine.

She smiled again, her slow, sweet smile, which spread like a ripple across her face, finally lighting up those dark blue eyes.

'My peace comes from accepting with thanks whatever God sends and, as he told us to do, rejoicing in all things.'

I gasped, her statement was so unexpected.

'But you have so little to rejoice about,' I protested.

'Rejoicing in the Lord does not depend on outside circumstances,' Ileana replied quietly, 'it depends on a person's relationship with Jesus.'

She looked up and her eyes were once again far away.

'When I had a lot of material things to rejoice over, I didn't rejoice,' she went on simply. 'Wealth and possessions, and I had both in abundance, bring their problems. Now life has stripped me of its trimmings and I am truly free because I have nothing left to lose down here.'

Looking round the bare room I certainly agreed with her there.

'Suffering burns up our shallowness,' she continued. 'It burnt up mine and showed me the truth.'

She leant back in her old armchair, her eyes and her thoughts still far away, and I held my breath, afraid of disturbing her, but longing to hear more.

'I have learned the difference between being devoted to a creed and being devoted to a person,' she said dreamily. 'All my life I had gone to Mass, done the right things, but it was only when disaster struck that I found peace . . . and Jesus.'

As she looked across at me her eyes were soft and translucent, shining like those of a young girl in love for the first time.

'Many a lost soul only finds God when he stops being religious,' she murmured, as if talking to herself. 'Jesus showed me his face and when that happened personal possessions, which I had lost anyway, became a matter of indifference to me, and I knew that the only thing that was important was my relationship to him.'

She paused again and the silence in the room was broken only by the bells of the Église Sainte Odile ringing the Angelus.

'My riches are now stored in heaven,' Ileana ended softly, 'where rust and decay cannot attack them.'

I was not a committed Christian when I first met her and I marvelled at her faith and her trust.

'But what do you do all day?' I remember enquiring quizzically.

She raised her eyebrows in surprise and I suddenly felt that my question was stupid.

'Although I haven't left this room for nearly twenty years,' she replied, 'I am very much aware of today's world and of the tensions and difficulties of present-day life. So now my days are filled with what, on the surface, may seem to some people to be all that is left to me, prayer and reaching out in love to you all. This prayer life, this communion I now have with Jesus, which I would never have found if I hadn't been stripped of everything I thought important, gives a sense and purpose to my life.'

At that time, early on in our friendship, I had thought that prayer was a means of getting what one wanted, a kind of Father Christmas list which we regularly presented to God – and it seemed to me that she had obtained very little. Perhaps she read my thoughts.

'You wonder why I am not bitter?' she queried. 'Why I say I have no regrets?'

I nodded, astonished at her perception.

'Because prayer to me,' she said quietly, 'is not to get answers, though that often happens, but to find a perfect oneness with God.'

She paused and propped her elbow on the table in front of her, idly brushing away the remaining crumbs with her free hand.

'You may think my life has been a failure,' she went on.

I started to protest but she interrupted me.

'You wouldn't be alone,' she smiled, 'many people do and, perhaps, in some ways, it has been.'

She paused again and this time her eyes looked straight into mine.

'But have you ever considered what a failure Jesus was?' she continued.

I caught my breath. Even to my 'churchgoer's' ears her words amounted almost to blasphemy.

'In the eyes of the world,' Ileana went on softly, 'socially, educationally, financially his life was a total failure . . . But from God's point of view it was a great success. To him, the only thing that was important was that Jesus had been obedient and done his Father's will.'

I nodded, gradually seeing what she meant.

'God's purposes are rarely man's purposes,' Ileana ended. 'Faith is not common sense and common sense is not faith. It is not a feeble sentiment either, but unswerving belief in the fact that God is love no matter what happens. I don't always understand what he is doing in my life but I know him, and that is what makes the difference.'

We sat for a few minutes in thoughtful silence.

'Had anyone told me when I was young and rich and healthy,' she mused, 'that this is how I would end my days, a penniless, crippled refugee living alone in one room, I don't think I would have wanted to live. Perhaps that is why in the

Bible God more than once condemns fortune tellers and says they are abhorrent in his sight. He does not want us to know the future, but to trust in him.'

Ileana paused, her eyes far away.

'Jesus was the only one who knew what the future held,' she continued so softly that I had to lean forward in order to catch her words, 'and only he could have had the courage to go ahead knowing how his earthly life would end. God, in his mercy, has spared us foreknowledge and forbidden us to seek it.'

She looked up from her musing and smiled, the same crinkly lines again fanning out around the bright luminous eyes.

'I leave my future in his hands,' she said serenely. 'Jesus has given me his peace.'

And it was this peace which shone through her. People of all kinds and creeds climbed the stairs to her attic room: the first time often out of duty sent by some voluntary organisation caring for the sick and needy or from her parish church, St Odile, whose steeple bells echoed round her bare room. But they always returned, not only out of duty but out of friendship, often bringing their own troubles and problems to share with her.

'Many of your visitors say they come here to escape for a short while from the pressures and turmoil of life and to try to capture some of your peace,' I smiled.

And, as I said it, I realised that the test of the life of a saint is not success, not even the number of rousing sermons they have preached or the lost souls they have brought to salvation. It is not success at all, in fact, but faithfulness to Jesus and his promises throughout their earthly life no matter what the circumstances. To show the glory of God, the life hidden in Jesus in any human condition and to spread his peace.

There was nothing dramatic about Ileana, in either her attitude to her faith or in her life, but there was something pure and beautiful, humbling to us who came to visit her, about her steadfast loyalty to God and her devotion to him in her daily walk.

In the Sermon on the Mount Jesus said: 'Blessed are the pure in heart', and in her poverty and her affliction, Ileana was truly blest. And, remembering her, I realise that it is so much easier to be a fanatic, someone who, like the Pharisees, is addicted not only to the law but to the letter of the law, and who pummels people into accepting their, often man-made, set of rules, rather than just to be a humble, faithful believer. The Pharisees were committed to religion, but Jesus was committed to people. Looking at Ileana's serene countenance, which bore the marks of deep suffering, I realised that through her love and her gentleness, not because of what she had said, she was the woman who had perhaps most influenced me in my turning to Jesus. Her peace was not dependent on material prosperity or on other people; it was the peace which Jesus left with his disciples and which he promises to all who believe in him.

And, to her dying day, Ileana truly had it. As she had lived those last thirty years, so she died. Knowing that she was accepted and loved by God had removed all fear from her life, the fear we all encounter when we meet Jesus at a deep level and look honestly at our lives, seeing ourselves as he sees us.

I'm glad that I had already committed my life to Jesus and had certainty of eternity before Ileana died, otherwise it would have been so painful to see the box containing the only externals I knew of her, her earthly body, being lowered into the damp, black earth that rainy December afternoon.

There would have been such anguish in my heart because there would have been no hope. But that grey afternoon I felt very little emotion. I knew that the body I had seen lying in the coffin was a body she no longer wanted or needed. It had caused her pain and as I looked down at her for the last time it wasn't Ileana's face I saw, it was the lifeless image which is all that remains when the spirit has departed. There seemed no longer to be any link between us because all earthly life had gone.

But I had assurance in my heart that that precious spirit had not been extinguished, that all she had stood for, all she represented in my life, had not gone forever, that one day we would meet again when that ageing body, which had become a nuisance to her, would be changed for a new body without pain, a beautiful new body which Jesus promises us at the final resurrection.

In I Corinthians 15 it says, when the body is buried it is mortal, when it is raised it will be immortal. When buried it is ugly and weak, when raised it will be beautiful and strong; when buried it is a physical body, when raised it will be a spiritual body.

But, in order for this to happen, there is one condition we must fulfil: we must believe in Jesus, be born again in him and receive his Holy Spirit, then as we read in Romans 8:

> If the Spirit of him who raised Jesus from the dead is living in you, he who raised Christ from the dead will also give life to your mortal bodies, through his Spirit, who lives in you.

For, as Jesus told us, before the flower can burst forth from the soil, alive and beautiful, the seed must first die and be buried in the earth.

Even her death was quiet and unspectacular and, like her Saviour, she was buried in a borrowed tomb, when one of the many friends who had visited her and been helped and strengthened by her over the years offered a place in her family vault. And it was there that Ileana's body was laid to rest on that damp, misty afternoon just before Christmas.

There were not many of us at the graveside and there was no church service simply because, in France, that adds to the cost. But I think Ileana would have preferred it that way, her faith so transcended the bounds of organised religion, it was everywhere in God's creation. Because of her infirmity she had not been inside a church for many years . . . and it had not been inside a church that she had met Jesus. Maybe the bleak silent graveyard under the bare trees was the right place to announce those words of everlasting life, to proclaim that her tired, crippled remains had now been changed into a glorious new body, and that Jesus had wiped away every tear from her eyes as she passed from death into his waiting arms.

A Dominican monk, one of her friends and a faithful visitor, a Rumanian refugee like herself, stood with us as her coffin was lowered into the grave and pronounced those wonderful words of hope which Jesus spoke to Martha as she grieved over her brother Lazarus' death:

I am the resurrection and the life, he who believes in me will live, even though he dies; and whoever lives and believes in me will never die.

As at Jesus's burial there were very few mourners and very little reverence. It was late afternoon and the gravediggers were anxious to get on with their work and be off. They sat on an adjacent tombstone and smoked, talking so loudly that the words of the short, simple service were barely audible.

Jacques turned round and asked them to lower their voices for a few minutes but, like the soldiers at the foot of the cross who divided up Jesus's clothes between them and threw dice for his robe as they waited for him to die, the gravediggers took no notice. As soon as the last words of that brief committal were uttered and the Dominican Father had replaced his white cowl on his damp head, they pushed by us with their shovels and began thudding the clogged black earth on to Ileana's coffin.

We turned away and walked slowly out of the Montmartre

cemetery where so many famous people have been laid to rest: Sacha Guitry, Théophile Gautier, Berlioz, Stendhal, Heine, Degas, Offenbach, people whose names had been famous on earth. But in heaven? Were their names written in the Lamb's Book of Life? Had they been part of the heavenly host waiting to greet Ileana, I wondered, as we passed the ornate tomb of Marie du Plessis, the model for Alexandre Dumas' famous novel *The Lady of the Camelias.*

I felt saddened at the way Ileana's funeral service had gone but knew that, to her, it would not have mattered at all. She had finally gone home to be with her Jesus and perhaps she was, even then, smiling her slow sweet smile which lit up her eyes so brightly – and laughing at us for minding. And I remembered her once saying to me:

'It is not where we die or where we are buried which is important, but who will be waiting to receive us when we get to the other side.'

She truly had turned her eyes upon Jesus, looked full in his wonderful face, and the things of earth had grown strangely dim in the light of his glory and grace.

Chapter 20

THEY COULD BE YOUR SONS OR MINE

Lights were springing up in the crowded thoroughfare and the short winter afternoon was drawing to a close as we stepped into the mass of Christmas shoppers hurrying along the streets of Montmartre. The contrast with the eerie stillness on the other side of the high stone cemetery walls was startling. The bare trees and the mist must have muffled the traffic noises and the cries of the street vendors behind their laden stalls.

Jacques took my arm and directed me towards the car.

'Etienne rang me this afternoon,' he said as he opened the door, and helped me in.

I looked up, still bewildered by the sudden stark contrast between the scene at the graveside and the outside reality.

'He's in Paris until tomorrow,' Jacques went on. 'I asked him for dinner this evening.'

I groaned with dismay; the last thing I wanted was a dinner party.

'Don't worry,' my husband soothed as he put the key in the ignition and began to manoeuvre out of the narrow parking space. 'I told him he'd have to take pot luck.'

'But . . .' I began.

'I tried to get hold of you but you'd already left when I rang.'

I made no comment.

'Now come on,' Jacques soothed, as I sat in silence. 'I know it's perhaps not the moment and I know how you're feeling, but you like Etienne and, anyway, it will take your mind off things.'

I sighed.

'I'm not going back to the office,' Jacques ended. 'I'll drive you home.'

It was true, I did like Etienne and normally would have been delighted to see him, but that evening, selfishly, I just wanted to be alone.

As we wound our way through the crowded noisy streets and then left Paris behind and headed towards the motorway and home I felt my spirits rise. Jacques had wisely made no attempt at conversation and I turned and put my hand over his on the wheel.

'Sorry,' I whispered.

He glanced down briefly at me and grinned.

'Feeling better?' he enquired.

'Mmmm,' I replied. 'What time is Etienne coming?'

'He said he'd ring as he was leaving,' Jacques replied, 'but I doubt whether it will be before eight, he seems to have a very heavy schedule.'

'Drugs?' I queried.

'I think so,' Jacques said quietly, 'he couldn't say much on the phone.'

Etienne was a Christian friend in the police force, who was very involved with the drug racket. As we sat together before the fire that evening after dinner, I looked across at him. He was a big man with the gentleness which big men so often have, but also a warmth, a depth and a kindness in his dark brown eyes.

He didn't look like a policeman.

I have always found the police to be very courteous and helpful but, as a rule, they are disliked by the general public in France and especially by the young people – I've never understood why. It seems to be deeply ingrained in the French character to mistrust and dislike the police force as a whole, to think that they are 'out to get them'. One rarely hears people speaking well of the police and children are not taught, as I was, that they are a tower of strength to turn to, to run to, if anything goes wrong.

As I poured the coffee I couldn't help thinking what a tower of strength Etienne would be to any child in trouble, to anyone in trouble, in fact.

'How long are you in Paris for this time, Etienne?' I enquired.

The firelight flickered on his rugged features and the lights from the Christmas tree just behind him were winking on and off, showing up the grey streaks in his thick dark hair, as he looked across at me and smiled.

'I hope only until tomorrow evening,' he said, leaning forward to put his coffee cup down on the low table in front of him. As he did so a sudden light from the tree stood out on the hair curling against the back of his neck.

'A quick trip,' Jacques cut in.

'Not quick enough for Colette,' Etienne laughed, mentioning his diminutive wife who barely came up to his armpits. 'After all, it *is* 21 December and she's terrified I won't get back for Christmas if this business drags. Then I really will be unpopular with the family.'

A shadow crossed his face and he sighed, 'But there'll be other mothers for whom Christmas won't be an occasion for rejoicing this year.'

I looked across at him, noticing the deep lines etched around his mouth.

'It must be hard to have your job,' I said sympathetically. 'I suppose, dealing with drugs, you have a lot to do with young people?'

'More and more, unfortunately,' he replied.

'How can you bear it?' I queried.

He looked across at me and there was sadness in his eyes.

'I couldn't,' he answered quietly, 'if all I was doing was arresting them and sending them for trial.'

'But isn't that what you have to do?' I pursued.

'Basically, yes,' he said. 'They have broken the law and are in deep trouble. But you know, they could be your sons or mine. They start taking drugs, often out of bravado at a party or because their friends do it, thinking they can handle it. And this is where it ends.'

I shivered, thinking of our children, realising that only by the grace of God were they, so far, saved from the horrors of drugs.

'But you can't have pity on those who deliberately corrupt others by peddling the stuff, can you?' I queried.

Etienne looked directly at me and his rugged face was serious.

'It may seem strange to you,' he answered quietly, leaning forward intently, 'but, oddly enough, I can. They are usually peddling because they are hooked themselves and need the money to satisfy their craving. It's a deadly, vicious circle.'

He passed his hand through his thick, dark hair.

'I always wonder what must have happened in their lives to make them turn to drugs in the first place and I ask myself what went wrong, what deep hurt they suffered somewhere along the way to make them as they are. After all, a baby is not born with habits, these are acquired and someone must have helped to form them.'

He sighed deeply and looked into the fire.

'The trouble with many of them,' he continued, 'is that they've never known love, all they've ever known is force and violence.'

The three of us sat in silence. I didn't know what to say, I had never considered criminals in that light at all and it made me think; of course they had once been babies, sweet helpless gurgling babies, they had once been someone's child.

'You know,' Etienne suddenly broke the silence, 'I've discovered that our ability to love others relates very closely to our experience of being loved. Many of these so-called criminals grew up in homes which were just battlefields, marital tragedies. Our children are so blessed, really blessed. Most of the young offenders I come in contact with can't even respond to love when it's shown them. They're so starved they simply don't know what it is.'

He laughed shortly.

'Rather like the youngsters born during the war refusing to eat bananas afterwards. They'd been deprived of them when they were small and so they were suspicious of them because they didn't know what they were. It's exactly the same thing.'

'But can you help them at all?' I enquired as his words sank in.

'I try,' Etienne replied quietly. 'Sometimes in the short time available there isn't a great deal I can do and it's hard, especially with the teenagers, to put handcuffs on them.'

He looked into the fire.

'I always see Thierry in their place,' he ended softly.

Thierry was Etienne and Colette's only son, a freshfaced boy of nineteen, the eldest of their four children.

'But what *can* you do?' I asked.

'Only one thing,' he said sadly. 'I look beyond what they've done and try to see them as Jesus sees them, as the people they can become through him, not the people they are now.'

He passed his hand distractedly through his thick dark hair.

'I try to show them that someone cares.'

He shook his head sadly.

'That doesn't mean that they don't have to pay the penalty for what they've done, but as the handcuffs are put on I place a New Testament in their hands. I always have copies in my desk, even in my pockets, and although it's not, strictly speaking, within police regulations, it's my way of saying "I hate the sin, but I love the sinner".'

My eyes were beginning to slowly fill with tears.

'And do they accept it?' I whispered.

'Mostly,' Etienne replied. 'They're young and, in spite of their swagger and their arrogance, deep down they're usually very frightened. Very few of them have any notion who Jesus is; and one I came across even thought he was a Brazilian football star! But I just hope that, when they are alone in their cell, they will open the New Testament and find comfort and hope ... and their Saviour.'

Like a metronome the twinkling lights on the Christmas tree flashed rhythmically on and off, lighting up the cosy room and, in this warm, peaceful atmosphere, the three of us sat in silence, gazing into the softly hissing fire, each busy with our own thoughts.

A log disintegrated and fell into the ashes, breaking the silence.

'It's a rum old world we've brought these youngsters into, isn't it?' Etienne said, picking up the thread of his thoughts almost as if he were talking to himself. 'There no longer appear to be any standards or values and they've nothing left to kick against, every barrier seems to collapse in front of them. I can't help wondering about the way we've failed them.'

I frowned. 'Surely not,' I began.

'I'm afraid yes,' Etienne went on. 'Many parents have shown this generation that the god they worship is materialism or money ... even violence. The young people must be so bewildered by the example we've given them that sometimes it doesn't surprise me that they turn away from it. All we've done is teach them the basic mechanics of living, temporary plumbing to last till something better turns up.'

Etienne looked across at me.

'Do you realise that in almost half the homes in this country it's not the parents who decide what is right for their children, but the judge? The children end up like a piece of meat which two dogs are fighting over, and a third party has to intervene and decide who's to have it. There are so many broken homes and remarriages that we're now living in the age of the wash-and-wear wedding dress. Marriage, instead of being a permanent relationship marked by love and trust and mutual support, no matter what the circumstances, has turned into a temporary battlefield.'

He sighed.

'It could explain why the world is in its present economic mess, and why our youngsters turn to drugs.'

We both looked at him enquiringly.

'I think that family solidarity is the root of national prosperity,' Etienne explained, 'and our national prosperity has had its roots brutally torn from the ground.'

He leant back in his chair and sighed.

'My heart aches for the young,' he said sadly. 'What standards or principles have we handed on to them?'

Etienne gazed into the fire, his long legs stretched out in front of him, then, as if coming back from a long way, he looked up and smiled at us.

'There are not many Christians in the police force,' he said sadly, 'but my staff know my convictions and, I think, respect them. At least I was led to believe so when one of them came to me a few months ago, after making a routine search of a prisoner's belongings before his transfer to another prison, and told me he had come across a New Testament. The prisoner told him he had received it when he was charged and that, whilst reading it in the weeks which followed, he had committed his life to Jesus and his whole attitude had changed. He was a young man with a stiff sentence to serve but he apparently had peace.'

Etienne smiled wryly.

'It's a tough life being a policeman. And one can either become hard and calloused by the broken lives one sees, or one can try to understand and do what one can to alleviate the suffering. But,' he ended, 'without Jesus I would find it impossible.'

The old clock in the hall wheezed and struck the half hour.

Etienne looked at his watch.

'I must be going,' he said. 'I've got to make an early start in the morning if I don't want to be in trouble with Colette. And

I shall be if I'm not on that last 'plane tomorrow night.'

We laughed, knowing Colette a radiant Christian who supported her husband wholeheartedly, we understood the pleasantry behind his words. But it must have been a long day for him, draining not only physically but mentally as he took upon himself the burdens of all those with whom he came in contact – burdens which had so often been too heavy for their young shoulders to carry. And I saw the whole situation in a different light and wondered, with Etienne, just what had happened in the lives of those young offenders which had hardened them and made them as they were.

As he rose from his chair I put my hand on his arm.

'Before you go,' I said quietly, 'let's just pray for those young people.'

Etienne looked at me and slowly lowered himself back into the armchair, bowing his dark head as he clasped his hands between his knees.

'Dear Lord,' he said softly, 'you only know what goes on in the heart of each one of us, you only can see the hidden depths, the pain, the fears, the bewilderment. And you taught us not to judge. Help us, Father, not to criticise or make hasty judgements on others, but just to see each person we come across as your child, made in your image. It's not easy, Jesus, and often it's impossible to imagine that some of them can have anything of you in them, their hearts have become so full of vice and hatred, their minds so warped.'

Etienne paused, then went on slowly.

'But Lord Jesus, let us never forget that you died for them as you died for us, that you came to heal not only the sick in body, but the sick in mind – and Lord how sick the minds of so many of those we meet every day have become. The task you gave us is impossible, Father, if we try to do it in our own strength. It is only by placing this tremendous burden on your shoulders that we can even begin to try to help. May we never forget that by ourselves we can do nothing, but that with you, Father, nothing is impossible. Jesus, only your love is inexhaustible, help us to love others from the depth of your love for us. May we stay so close to you, be so identified with you, that your love and sweetness are poured out through us incessantly. The world is so thirsty, Father: help us to be your fountain of life.'

The tears were now flowing down my cheeks. I thought of our own children, happy and carefree, looking forward to our family Christmas, to the New Year celebrations with their friends. I thought of myself, so blessed in my home and my family, and my heart went out to those other mothers whose boys, just as precious to them as mine were to me, were now lying frightened and alone in a prison cell awaiting trial. And, as Jacques began to pray, although the words wouldn't come my voice was so choked, in my heart I prayed that Jesus would come to these lost souls, would send one of his servants to comfort them, and that in the silence and solitude of their prison cells, these young men would turn to the Word of Life which Etienne had given them and find Jesus.

As we rose to say goodbye I realised once again what that small seed, that tiny grain of truth, just scattered, apparently at random can do. That it can be the beginning of an immense harvest and we must never lose any opportunity to spread God's Word, to tell others about Jesus and what he has done in our lives.

They may be indifferent, they may change the subject, they may even appear not to be listening, but Jesus has given us his solemn command to go into the world and spread the good news, and we have no option but to do it. We may never know how many have heard or how many have found the truth because of us not, that is, until we reach heaven and they come to tell us themselves.

For me, Etienne who so towered above me, epitomised the phrase 'a man never stands so tall as when he kneels to help a child'. He will never know on this earth how many lost children he helped, but I am sure that when he finally comes face to face with his God he will meet a crowd of witnesses, young men and old who, but for his faithfulness, would have been lost.

And he will hear his Saviour say:

'Well done, my good and faithful servant.'

Chapter 21

REBELLION

In the busy, action-packed days which followed Etienne's visit and preceded our family Christmas I was strangely troubled. It wasn't only sadness over Ileana's death, which I knew to be not only stupid but totally unreasonable, it was more than that.

Etienne's visit and our conversation had disturbed and upset me. It had shown me another world of which I was only vaguely conscious through newspapers and the television, a world I had preferred not to think about because I found it upsetting. And, much as I liked him, I wished he hadn't come that particular day, when I was feeling so emotional anyway, and that the subject we had discussed had not been raised.

As a mother, I began to wonder about this world into which I had brought my children and, like all mothers when they really face up to the nitty-gritty of the present day, I felt afraid.

We all want so much for them, we hurt when they hurt and perhaps our greatest burden is that we cannot suffer for them, as those mothers who knew their sons to be behind bars, whilst all around them was the rush and bustle and the joyful anticipation of Christmas, would no doubt willingly have done. But, unfortunately, as they grow older and test their wings, as they struggle with the pains and problems of growing up, we can no longer say as we did in the past when a task was defeating them, 'give it to me, I'll do it for you.' We have to let them learn by their own mistakes and are so often helpless when we see them taking what we know to be the wrong turning.

All we can do is hand them over to Jesus and pray that they will learn, through those mistakes, and return in time to the right path. And I wondered how many mothers, sorrowing for their children at that moment, had been able to do just that – had that personal relationship with Jesus which allowed them to do so.

It's easy to hand them over when things are going well, in the same way as it is then easy to have faith. But when disaster strikes, as mothers we find it almost impossible to believe that Jesus really does love our precious children even more than we do. Or, at least, I did.

Maybe my Lord, in bringing Etienne to dinner that December evening and steering our conversation towards adolescent problems, was preparing me for the drama which lay ahead. I don't know. But our happy family Christmas was no sooner over than I ran headlong into a deadlock situation: Yves' particularly explosive teenage rebellion.

We had gone through it, more or less dramatically, with the three elder ones and survived, but with Yves it was different and made it seem as if our whole world was rocking. What I didn't realise was that *his* whole world was rocking too and, whereas at least Jacques and I had each other to turn to for comfort and consolation, he was alone in this terrible mental turmoil.

I couldn't understand his behaviour. I couldn't understand why he didn't want to conform, why he wanted to throw over all we had brought him up to believe in, all our standards, and take what I was convinced was the rocky road to disaster. But Jesus understood and he taught me so much as we ploughed the furrow of this particular problem together. Had I not been yoked to him I really wonder whether I would have survived, for the burden was very heavy, both emotionally and physically, but God proved his faithfulness in bringing strength out of weakness.

During that fraught year I felt my strength, my own puny earthly strength draining away, as I faced this beloved child, this highly sensitive idealistic young boy who had almost become a stranger to me.

With hindsight I see that the rumblings had started much earlier than I thought, around his sixteenth birthday, in fact, when he began to crawl out of the chrysalis which had cocooned him until then and seek to fly for himself ... and it almost ended in disaster. Disaster because I was trying to pour him into a mould, my mould, a mould I had chosen for him. It wasn't until later that I realised that children are not jellies; they can't be poured into a shape and allowed to set, not, that is, if one wants satisfactory results.

I thought I had learned that lesson with the others, but how slow we mothers sometimes can be to understand. Perhaps we are not entirely to blame for each child is different and approaches adolescence in his or her own way.

That year of Yves' rebellion was a bad year for his school. There was great unrest, leading to lightning strikes by the teaching staff, and frustration and dissatisfaction on the part of the pupils. I had mentioned to the headmaster, at a parents' meeting just before Etienne's visit, that the situation seemed neither satisfactory nor healthy and that I was becoming increasingly worried by Yves' antagonistic attitude towards the whole school set-up. But he had assured me that I was worrying unnecessarily and, as no parent likes to be considered a 'mother hen', especially where teenage sons are concerned, I had said no more.

Jacques was very busy professionally at the time and often away and, when I had mentioned that Yves didn't seem happy and that I was sure things weren't as they should be at school he, like the headmaster, had soothed me and told me it was all part of growing up. And, once again, I had allowed myself to be lulled into a false sense of security until that Monday evening when the telephone rang at ten o'clock, an almost unheard of thing in France where, except in cases of emergency, no one rings after nine-thirty.

When I picked up the receiver it was like an icy shower.

'We've discovered that your son is leading a group of strikers on a march from the school tomorrow morning, madame,' the headmaster announced. 'Would you please prevent him from doing this.'

I suddenly went numb.

'I can't believe it,' I gasped.

'I'm afraid it's true,' he said coldly. 'We've just had an emergency meeting and your son is the ring leader.'

Prickles of anger replaced the goose pimples and began to slowly creep up my back as my lips tightened into a hard line.

'Isn't it a little late to appeal to me?' I asked through clenched teeth.

There was a moment's astonished silence; in France headmasters are not accustomed to being challenged.

'I beg your pardon?' he enquired, obviously not believing his ears.

I breathed heavily.

'If you remember, at the meeting last term I mentioned to you that I was not happy about Yves; that there were rumblings of a kind I didn't like and I was afraid of what might happen.'

He didn't immediately reply.

'I think that you are shutting the gate after the horse has bolted,' I said grimly, 'but I'll see what I can do.'

He seemed a little chastened.

'If you would,' he answered. 'Perhaps you could be at the school a little before eight o'clock, that is when they are planning to set off.'

'I hope it won't be necessary,' I replied tightly.

'So do I,' he ended.

And we hung up.

I knew that Yves was asleep and I didn't see any point in waking him. I thought about telephoning Jacques, but he was in Germany and I didn't see what he could do, except comfort me, and I needed more than comfort at that time.

Yves couldn't have chosen a worse moment. With his father away I felt amputated and helpless, totally unable to cope with this crisis on my own.

As I tossed and turned, unable to sleep, I realised that when Yves began rebelling against 'authority' and what he called the petty tyranny of the teachers, causing him to question many things and as a consequence lean towards anarchy, he had obviously been terribly influenced by the teachers themselves – who had been holding one day strikes ever since September, thoroughly disrupting the students' work and making any routine impossible for them.

When finally, exhausted by anger, shock and sheer frustration, I fell into a fitful sleep I heard myself crying: 'Oh Lord, what has happened to that lovely boy who once knew you? Why has he turned away? What has gone wrong?'

The next morning when Yves came down to breakfast I didn't know what to do. As the clock ticked away the minutes my throat constricted, knowing that Christopher, who started school half an hour later than his brother, would soon be down and I didn't want him to be involved in what was happening. As Yves gulped down the last of his hot chocolate I looked across the table at him and my eyes filled with tears. He was so young, so vulnerable and yet . . .

'Don't do it Yves,' I whispered. 'Please don't do it.'

He stopped drinking and looked up over the rim of his cup, his eyes startled.

'The headmaster telephoned late last night,' I gulped, tears stinging at the back of my eyes. 'He says you're leading a strike.'

I dropped my eyes as the tears began to slowly roll down my cheeks.

'Please don't,' I said brokenly, 'please don't.'

And, hardly knowing what I was doing, I put my hands over my eyes as huge sobs began to heave up from the depths of my being.

Yves abruptly put down his cup and came across to where I was sitting. He put his arm round my shoulder and I reached up a wet hand and squeezed his gratefully, imagining that I had won. But I had not bargained for my son's iron will, the iron curtain of resistance which had been building up between the two of us over the past months.

He bent and kissed my cheek.

'Please don't cry, Mum,' he murmured. 'Please... I... I have to go.'

And, withdrawing his arm, he grabbed his things and left.

His words stunned me and as I remembered Etienne's recent visit they crashed like an icy wave through my brain, sending terrifying pictures flashing through my mind. My immediate reaction was to give way to a fresh, overwhelming flow of tears and self-pity which were both there just beneath the surface, threatening to submerge me, but I heard Christopher clattering down the stairs. Quickly blowing my nose and scrubbing my hankie round my wet face, I got up from the table, my back deliberately turned towards our youngest son.

'Your breakfast's on the table, darling,' I said, trying to force a note of normality into my shaking voice. 'I've got to rush out, won't be long, but I expect you'll have left before I get back.'

I felt Christopher's eyes on me as I left the dining room but I dared not turn around and show my face and, surprisingly, he said nothing. Maybe he knew why I was leaving, perhaps he knew far more about his brother's activities than I did. It seemed that everybody knew but me.

Yves' words 'I have to go' rang in my ears as I walked with the dogs through the drizzling rain to school that dark February morning.

He had sounded as if he were being driven by a force outside himself, stronger than himself, almost against his will and the implications which had shot into my mind at the breakfast table suddenly framed themselves into the one dreaded word I'd refused to even contemplate: *drugs*.

'Oh no,' I cried out loud, as I stopped dead in my tracks, rooted to the spot, suddenly feeling drained and exhausted and quite incapable of going on, incapable of any reaction at all. 'Oh no, it can't be that. Not Yves.'

But the dogs were pulling and tugging at their leads and my feet began to mechanically move forward till, in a daze, I found myself at the school gate.

It was just beginning to get light. The headmaster was there with those members of his staff who were not on strike. They seemed pitifully few, backed by various representatives from parent-teacher associations and a milling mass of senior pupils carrying home-made banners.

The headmaster looked stonily at me, obviously realising that I had failed. His depleted staff didn't exactly look as if they were bursting with understanding, either. I gazed back with the same stony expression each of us, I think, blaming the other for what had happened.

'Where's Yves?' I enquired tightly.

Without answering, the headmaster looked over my head and waved his arm vaguely into the crowd, towards the banners.

I caught a glimpse of some of Yves' friends on the other side of the road, but I still couldn't see my son. I began to panic and ran across to where they were standing, the one word, DRUGS, still hammering a tattoo in my brain.

'Laurent,' I shouted, grabbing one of the boys by the arm, 'what are you doing? Where's Yves?'

He looked down at me and smiled. He was a nice boy, one of Yves' best friends, an idealist like my son.

'Over there, madame,' he said, pointing to where a mass of other banners were gathered. 'We're just about to set off.'

'Don't do it,' I pleaded. 'Don't do it... please.'

I turned frantically to his companion holding the other end of the banner, another regular visitor to our house.

'Please, Bruno, please don't do it,' I almost sobbed. 'Give it up, you can't get anywhere, it's crazy.'

But Bruno only gave me the same polite smile I had received from Laurent.

'I'm sorry, madame,' he said gently, turning away as the two of them and their home-made banner moved out into the road.

A short, stocky boy who had not greeted me stepped into place beside them. I suddenly recognised him. He was the only son of one of the village women who had worked for me some years before. I had known him almost before he was born, his mother had brought him to my house in his carry-cot and now she worked at the local baker's to help keep him at school.

I grabbed him by the coat.

'Yannick, how *dare* you,' I screamed, now absolutely beside myself. 'How *dare* you. Your mother is working all hours to give you an education and this is how you repay her.'

But he merely pulled himself away from me and was swallowed up in the crowd.

As the students walked past me I stood with the tears streaming down my cheeks. I was now convinced that my son was on drugs but mercifully I was wrong. I had merely come up against teenage idealism and dedication with a vengeance, less permanently damaging than drugs but very painful, and even dangerous whilst it lasts.

I walked slowly back up the hill to the house, anger, fear, frustration and utter helplessness now overwhelming me, and I suddenly felt furious with the whole world. With the school for what they had done to my precious son, with my husband for not being there when I needed him and finally with God to whom I had given this child: I felt he had let me down.

In my misery and self-pity I forgot that God also gave us free will, and he will never force us if we reject him and choose to go the wrong way.

I entered the house drained and unhappy but, as I sat down at the cluttered breakfast table and put my head in my hands, I heard the words: 'He is my child: you gave him to me. Leave the matter in my hands.'

And once again the tears began to flow. But they were cleansing tears, even healing tears, bringing peace, that peace which our Lord promises and which I had lost in the turmoil simply because, like Peter when he stepped out of the boat and walked on the water towards Jesus, I had taken my eyes off the master and, in so doing, become aware of the raging waves all around me. And, like Peter, I had almost drowned.

That peace was still with me when Yves returned home late in the afternoon, drenched, his face drawn with fatigue. He looked at me warily but as I smiled and said my usual, 'Hallo darling', he came over to where I was sitting and hugged me, and I breathed a sigh of relief, thinking the matter was now closed.

But it wasn't. It was only the beginning.

Had it ended there perhaps the school might have agreed to ignore the whole incident but, after that first student march when they had completely stopped the traffic in the neighbouring town as pupils from other lycées left school to join them, matters went from bad to worse. It seemed that whenever the pupils did go to school the teachers were on strike and vice versa.

I still hadn't gathered what the students were striking for and wonder if they really knew themselves. Their home-made banners which carried slogans demanding that they be treated as individuals and not 'things' seemed so vague. Having seen the stony faces of the headmaster and his staff and the complete lack of communication between them and the pupils helped me to see that perhaps Yves and his friends did have a grievance, but I also realised that striking was *not* the answer.

But how could I tell Yves to obey the teachers, follow their example, when the teachers themselves were behaving in an anarchistic manner and striking most of the time themselves?

The matter really came to a head between Yves and me one afternoon a few weeks later when I thought he was in school and I suddenly saw him in the neighbouring town on his way to yet another protest meeting in their lycée. My flimsily veiled acceptance of the situation boiled over the top and I leapt out of the car and grabbed him. He resisted and we had a slanging match there on the pavement in the midst of the afternoon shoppers and the bus queue. We were both beside ourselves with rage. I don't know what the passers-by must have thought, but just as some very nasty words were bubbling to my lips in reply to some pretty hurtful things Yves had slung at me, the rage fused and subsided as the words: 'He is my child. Leave the matter in my hands' followed by: 'Hate the sin, but love the sinner' came into my mind. And, as I faced Yves across the sea of rebellion, I heard myself speak calmly to him.

'I hate the way you're behaving, but you're my son and no matter what you do I'll always love you.'

Yves opened his mouth, then closed it, took one long, hard look at me and turned on his heel and left.

Perhaps those words which Jesus put into my mouth were more effective than my anger or my pleading. I don't know. But I think that that was the turning point for him. Maybe he needed, maybe all rebellious youth need, the absolute assurance that although the world rejects them or appears to reject them, like Jesus those who truly love them, with his unconditional Calvary love, never will.

I know Yves needed that assurance in the months ahead because, although he passed easily into the class above, at the end of the summer term the school notified us that he would not be admitted the following September.

I'm sure he was upset by his expulsion, though he said very little, but he flatly refused to go to a private school and we knew that, at seventeen, it would be useless to force him. So, having tried everything to make him see reason, our kind of reason, and failed, we now did what we should have done months before: his father and I sat down with him and asked him what he really wanted to do. And, after all those months of anger, rebellion and frustration on his part and tears, pleading and tension on mine, communication was re-established, the floodgates opened and all his resentment and pent-up emotions came pouring out.

We did understand his dislike of the rigid division between staff and pupils which exists in French lycées, the lack of communication and the fact that schools then, and perhaps even now, are institutions where knowledge is fed into the pupils and that is all, without any great regard for the differences in pace, maturity or interests of the pupils themselves.

Perhaps I understood better than Jacques, who had been through the system and survived; but his father and I both agreed that opting out was not the answer. We knew that Jesus was... Jesus who had changed the world without fighting any battles. But Yves had turned away and was seeking the truth for himself.

We finally agreed, with great misgivings on our part though we tried to be positive, to allow him to start a school with some of his friends run on the liberal lines of A. S. Neill whose book, *Summerhill*, seemed to have replaced the Bible in Yves' life. And, from that moment on, our relationship with Yves changed and the tensions disappeared from him and from our family life.

Jacques and I had tremendous doubts about the wisdom of such a venture, but we realised that if we wanted to keep contact with Yves we had no choice, at this stage, but to give in. We were completely honest with him, telling him that we didn't understand his attitude or his ideas, but that we loved him and would support him on the understanding that, if it didn't work, he would have the courage to tell us and let us help him to find another solution.

So the following September, when all their friends went back to the lycée, Yves and nine other 'rebels' settled down to work in the room the local youth club had lent them and which they had spent the summer decorating, painting all the bits of furniture they had salvaged from family attics, in bright, eye-catching colours.

They named it the Parallel School and studied by themselves on work set by teachers who were sympathetic to their cause and came to give them lessons when they could. And, in spite of all our apprehensions, it worked! Yves was so much more relaxed and happy than he had been the year before and seemed to expand mentally.

Through this trauma I humbly acknowledged that, in spite of outward appearances and all my self-pity and anger against God, Jesus did have his hand on my son and was guiding him, although Yves did not know it or acknowledge it. I'm sure God did not intend Yves to be a rebel but, as the Bible says, in Romans 8:28: 'And we know that in all things God works for the good of those who love him, who have been called according to his purpose.' Our Lord in his infinite wisdom is able to take our mistakes and turn them into something positive, create something good out of evil. He finally turned Yves' rebellion and expulsion into channels which were right for him.

As I surfaced from this experience Jesus showed me in prayer one morning that our son had not lost *his* faith; he had lost *our* faith, his father's and mine, and had turned away to seek the truth for himself for, like eternal life, faith is not something we are born with or can inherit. It is a personal encounter with Jesus, a decision each one of us must make, whether to believe in him or not.

But our Lord's words 'seek and you will find' comforted me and gave me peace, and since that day when I 'let go ... and let God', when I took my hands off my teenage son and not only believed but claimed God's promise, that if I left the matter in his hands he would guide Yves' life, I have felt at peace about his future. And even though at the time he appeared to be hurtling towards disaster, Jesus stooped down and rescued him and gave him back to us in a new, deeper, more loving relationship than I had ever believed possible.

I have met many Christian parents who can testify to the same experience. But few people have had their faith in God's good purposes for their children tested to the limits endured by Ruth and Harold Miller. Jacques and I first met their daughter Stephanie the winter after our traumatic experience with Yves, at a seminar we attended in Switzerland. Her story is a remarkable one...

Chapter 22

MAKE ME A LADY

'Mother,' said Stephanie miserably as she sat at the kitchen table, her pretty face cupped in her hands. 'Why can't I be small and dainty like other girls. Why did I have to grow so tall?'

Ruth Miller looked round from the sink where she was slicing carrots into a large pan and smiled at her daughter.

'Because God likes you that way,' she replied quietly.

Stephanie jumped to her feet and kicked back the stool, her violet eyes blazing with anger.

'Well, I don't like him... anyway,' she flung over her shoulder as she slammed from the room.

Ruth leant against the sink and closed her eyes. Stephanie was their only daughter, a pretty girl with chestnut curls, but at fourteen she measured six feet three. Ruth knew that her daughter was suffering, but she was powerless to help her.

'Oh Jesus, watch over her,' she prayed. 'We've brought her up to know you and love you but now I'm afraid for her – this hurt goes very deep.'

Deeper perhaps than anyone realised.

At sixteen Stephanie left home, and although her parents did everything they could to find her, she cut all links with her family and turned to drugs, gradually sinking lower and lower as she sought to satisfy her craving.

'You could get off drugs and get a job,' a little remnant of her conscience sometimes whispered to her. 'You're attractive and there are plenty of tall girls around ... You could even go back home, they still love you,' it finally cajoled.

But Stephanie's rebellion against God, her parents and society was total. Her height had become an obsession with her; she dreamed of being five feet nothing and tripping along on stiletto heels and was incapable of accepting herself as she was. Drugs became her escape from reality.

Eventually her craving proved too expensive for her to handle, but there were men around who were willing to help and she turned to the oldest profession. Stephanie was by now so completely hooked on drugs that she felt there was no way of escape, yet sometimes she longed to go back home, to be a little girl again. She knew, even without that small voice inside which kept reminding her, that her parents still loved her and would do anything to help her but, every time her resolve began to crumble, she would remember her mother's calm acceptance of her daughter's obsession and hear her voice saying: 'God likes you that way.'

And a blinding uncontrollable rage would take hold of Stephanie. In her bitterness she blamed the world, God, her parents, society ... and there was still the terrible craving to be satisfied.

One night she and two other drug addicts decided to hold up and rob a jeweller's shop.

She was caught: the other two managed to get away and left her to face the trial alone. Stephanie was just eighteen when she was convicted of armed robbery and sentenced to eight years in prison.

'Stephanie,' her mother called brokenly as she was led from the court.

Her daughter looked round, then quickly looked away again, refusing to meet her parents' eyes, or even acknowledge them as, with his arm round his stricken wife, Harold Miller left the court. But they didn't give up. Every visiting day found them outside the prison gates, often unable even to see her, and they kept praying that God would work a miracle of healing in their daughter's heart.

Prison seemed to bring out all the anger and rebellion in Stephanie and she served half her sentence in solitary confinement, locked alone in an almost empty underground cell for thirty days at a time – the maximum period allowed for solitary confinement – after she had attacked a wardress or got into a brawl with another prisoner.

'I hated solitary confinement and yet I wanted it at the same time,' she confessed afterwards. 'When I was alone in that bare cell I didn't see myself towering above everyone any more. I used to live in a fantasy dream world, imagining that I was small and feminine, that I had a beautiful home with chandeliers in every room and a big tall husband who adored me. I longed to be a lady, but God had made me a carthorse and I hated him.'

And each time she was punished and put in that lonely cell she sank deeper and deeper into make-believe, unwilling to return to the 'normality' of everyday prison life.

The day she left prison, having served seven of her eight year sentence, she was just twenty-five. Her parents were outside the gates, waiting for her.

'Stephanie,' pleaded her mother, 'come home, just for a little while, you need time.'

'I've done time,' her daughter replied grimly, 'now I'm not going to waste it. You stick to your praying and let me get on with my life; I want the bright lights not the altar candles. I don't need God and I don't need you either.'

And with a false bravado which had come to be her armour against a world she felt had wronged her, she went back to her old ways.

A strip-club welcomed her. Her height wasn't a problem and seven years in prison had hardened her. She went to share a flat with three other girls from the club where drugs and men were their daily pattern. Then one dreary winter afternoon when she was alone the telephone rang and, picking up the receiver, she heard a man's voice on the other end of the line.

'I'd like to come and talk to you,' he said quietly.

'Sure, sweetheart, come on round,' cooed Stephanie as with a yawn she climbed off the sofa and began emptying overflowing ashtrays and gathering up the dirty glasses scattered around the room.

But the young man who arrived on the doorstep wasn't like the usual clients. Stephanie curled back on to the sofa and pushed a whisky bottle towards him.

'No, thank you,' he said quietly, 'I don't drink.'

'Please yourself,' she replied, lighting a cigarette and tossing the packet in his direction. 'I suppose you're going to tell me you don't smoke either?'

'Quite right,' he answered. 'I don't.'

'What do you do?' she asked coyly, letting her housecoat fall away as she stretched out her long slender legs.

But he didn't seem to notice.

'I tell people about Jesus.'

For a moment Stephanie was too stunned to reply then, quickly recovering herself, she threw back her head and roared with laughter.

'Oh no,' she gasped, 'not that. You've come to the wrong house, chum.'

But he merely leant back in his chair and crossed his legs, his deep-set eyes never leaving her face.

'No,' he went on quietly, 'I haven't.'

Stephanie stopped laughing and her mouth tightened.

'Do you know what sort of a place this is?' she hissed. 'Do you know what I do?'

'You work in a strip-club,' he answered evenly.

Those steady grey eyes fixed on her were disconcerting.

'But do you know what I do for extra money – here? What we all do to be able to buy dope?'

'The same as Mary Magdalene did,' he replied calmly, 'and she came to love Jesus.'

For a moment Stephanie was shattered then a sudden rage overtook her and she leapt off the sofa.

'Get out of here before I throw something at you,' she

yelled, her violet eyes blazing with hatred.

'I don't mind if you throw something at me,' he smiled. 'I'm good at ducking.'

But Stephanie was not amused.

'Mister,' she said menacingly, 'I've met your sort before and you make me sick. Now go.'

The young man got up with a smile.

'All right,' he said cheerfully, 'I'll go, but I'd like to come back...'

'Get...out,' said Stephanie tightly through clenched teeth.

As the door closed quietly behind him she took a large gulp of neat whisky and turned on the stereo full blast. Those unwavering grey eyes had disturbed her; his calm, his gentleness, his lack of guile reminded her of her father and of the people she had known as a child and long since rejected. And she didn't want to be reminded.

As she slumped down in an armchair a sudden feeling of utter misery swept over her and tears began to trickle down her painted cheeks and, although she wouldn't admit it, something had begun to melt inside Stephanie.

Brushing her tears aside she picked up a magazine from the low cluttered table in front of her and, as she did so, a piece of paper fluttered from it and fell to the floor. Automatically she stooped to pick it up.

'Jesus came into the world to save sinners,' sprang out at her.

Incredulously she turned the paper over and the words 'Jesus loves you' stared up at her from the other side.

Angrily she threw the leaflet to the floor and stamped her foot on it. But the arrow had struck home and Stephanie was unable to find any semblance of peace.

A few nights later as she left the club in the early hours of the morning he fell into step beside her.

'May I walk home with you?' he enquired.

'Get the hell out of here,' she hissed.

But he seemed not to hear and, taking her arm, walked

easily at her side chatting about nothing in particular. Stephanie didn't resist. It was comfortable to have him there, knowing that there were no strings attached to his light touch on her arm. It dawned on her that he was interested in her as a person, not as a body, not for what he could get out of her. And suddenly, she didn't feel so tall any more.

When they reached her door he held out his hand for her key and without knowing why she did so she gave it to him, standing meekly at his side as he opened the door, and then handed it back to her.

'Goodnight, Stephanie,' he said gently, 'sleep well... and God bless you.'

And he was gone.

She stood as if in a dream listening to his light step become more and more distant as he ran down the stairs then, like a sleepwalker, turned and went into her flat. Sitting down in an armchair she put her hand in her coat pocket, feeling for a cigarette.

Out came another piece of paper.

'Whoever finds me finds life.'

As if mesmerised, she turned it over.

'Lo, I stand at the door and knock. If any man hear my voice...'

'Oh no,' she cried brokenly, as tears began to make channels down her cheeks.

The next night she half expected to see him, but he wasn't there and Stephanie felt a sharp sense of disappointment. When the night after he still didn't appear, she felt as if she had been tricked.

'What the hell,' she said irritably as she let herself into the flat and slumped in a chair, kicking off her shoes. 'As if I cared.'

And she reached for a cigarette. But she did care. On the third day the doorbell rang again and there he was on the landing.

'May I come in?' he smiled.

She just stood there.

'Stephanie,' he said gently as he walked uninvited into the flat, 'let me tell you how you can find true happiness, how your life can be changed and you can know lasting joy and peace.'

And he took her arm and led her to a chair. Stephanie was in a daze, she didn't seem to be in control of her body any more.

'Why do you plaster your face with all that stuff?' he asked quietly.

But she just continued to stare at him.

'Your eyes are a beautiful violet blue, but they don't go with that straw coloured hair; in fact, nothing goes with anything any more ... does it?' he enquired gently. 'Why don't you take off the mask you're hiding behind and just be yourself?'

She still said nothing, but her hand strayed to the lank blonde curls which hung to her shoulders.

'It's because you don't like yourself as you are, isn't it?' he continued.

She nodded, still unable to speak.

'But God loves you ... just as you are,' he went on quietly. 'He made you in his image.'

Stephanie put her face in her hands and started to cry uncontrollably, great sobs heaving her body as tears squeezed through her fingers and trickled up her bare arm.

He waited until the storm had passed.

'That's where it all started,' she sobbed. 'That's what my mother answered when I asked her why I was so tall – "God likes you that way", and it was the beginning of the end for me. I couldn't accept a God who could let me go through all the torments I'd had at school because of my height.'

Stephanie gave a great shuddering sob.

'I have the same feelings as dainty little girls,' she cried pitifully. 'Kids at school can be pretty cruel ...' she whispered, almost to herself.

The young man leaned across and held out his handkerchief, his eyes full of compassion. 'Sometimes God has to stand by and watch us go through difficult waters in order to bring us to him,' he said gently.

'It didn't bring me to him,' she said fiercely. 'It turned me away.'

'That's only part of the story,' he continued evenly, 'we haven't got to the end yet. Tell me honestly, are you really happy living this life?'

She shook her head.

'Wouldn't you like to change and become a lady?'

The word hit just where it was meant to. Be a lady: that was what she had always dreamed of. And for a fleeting second she saw a glimmer of hope before despair clamped down again. Ladies were always five feet nothing.

'It's too late,' she said through clenched teeth. 'I can't go back now.'

'No,' he agreed, 'by yourself you can't, but with God's help you can, and he's just waiting and longing to help you. Won't you let him?'

Suddenly something snapped inside Stephanie and the dream faded.

'Leave me alone,' she cried angrily. 'Get out of here and leave me alone; don't you know I'm hooked? I can't get through the day without a fix. No one can get off drugs without going through hell. They gave me the cold turkey treatment in prison and I'm not prepared to suffer that kind of torture again.'

Stephanie jumped to her feet but he was there beside her.

'No one can come off drugs by themselves,' he answered calmly, 'but with God all things are possible.'

And dropping to his knees he quietly began to pray.

'Oh Father,' he said softly, 'let Stephanie know you love her and that her sins have been forgiven by your son's death on the cross. Open her eyes so that she can see you and feel your presence and your peace and, yes, your power in her life. Fill her with your Spirit and lift from her this dreadful craving which is eating away at her body and her mind; Jesus deliver her from this evil today, bring her into your presence and . . . make her a lady.'

He stopped and remained kneeling, his head bowed.

Almost without realising what she was doing Stephanie had slipped to her knees beside him, the tears once again cascading down her cheeks and falling on to the stained carpet. But they were healing tears, washing away the hurt and the bitterness which had filled her heart. He reached for her hand and held it tightly.

'Just tell Jesus that you love him and you're sorry,' he pleaded. 'Tell him you want him to come into your life.'

'I'm sorry,' she whispered over and over again. 'Jesus, I'm sorry and if you're real I want you in my life, I want to be free from these drugs, I want to be washed clean and . . . be a lady.'

They remained kneeling in silence When Stephanie looked up a wonderful light seemed to have flooded the tawdry flat, an immense joy and peace filled her whole being, she knew that Jesus had answered her prayer and that she had been forgiven. That she was now a child of God and he had . . . made her a lady.

That was eleven years ago.

Stephanie was delivered off drugs on the spot.

And not only was her prayer answered but those of her parents also, for Ruth and Harold Miller now have a daughter again.

That evening of her conversion she returned to the strip-club for the last time and, when all those with whom she had worked since leaving prison were gathered together, she told them quietly and simply, without any exaggeration or undue emotion, exactly what had happened to her that afternoon: how she had accepted Jesus Christ as her personal Saviour and, as the Bible promised, been ransomed, healed, restored, forgiven, absolutely cleansed and made a new creature in him.

'In spite of my past,' she said quietly, 'I feel that he has made me a virgin again.'

As soon as she left the strip-club she began sharing her new-found faith with prostitutes, starting with those round about whom she knew.

'That was the hardest time of all,' she said, 'going back to my old haunts, to the people who had known me as I once was and trying to convince them that Jesus had really come into my life and made me a new creature in him.'

But Jesus understood her difficulty, for he had faced the same opposition himself when he returned to Nazareth and began to preach in the Temple there. Although the people were astonished at his wisdom and the words that fell from his mouth they were offended and said: 'He's no better than we are. He's just a carpenter, Mary's boy and a brother of James and Joseph, Judas and Simon.'

And Jesus had replied, no doubt with great sorrow, for he was trying to bring them his message of hope, 'A prophet is honoured everywhere except in his own home town.'

And he led Stephanie on to work with ex-prisoners.

When we first met Stephanie just a few years after her dramatic conversion, Jacques and I found it almost impossible to believe that this fresh-complexioned, bubbling young woman with the beautiful clear blue eyes and shining chestnut curls had once been a loud-mouthed, metallic blonde, a brawling prisoner, a gang member, a drug addict and a prostitute. She now carried her height with pride and her burning love for Jesus and her eagerness to share what he had done for her, the miracle of transformation he had effected in her life, were not only refreshing and inspiring to witness but also very moving to hear about.

Her dream was to open a half-way house where, before going back to face the world, women leaving prison could learn a new way of life and hear about the God who had created them and who loves them . . . just as they are.

When we met her for the second time a few years later her dream had come true and three such houses had been opened where 'my girls', as she called them, were helped to adjust to the outside world; but a different world from the one they had once known, a world where Jesus was now guiding their lives, a world in which they had the assurance that they were special and precious to him and had a right to be there.

I think God brought Stephanie into our lives when he did to prove to us just how faithful he is, how he does answer prayer and how we can confidently leave our children in his hands.

Like Yves, Stephanie had been brought up in a Christian home, taken to church and Sunday School and, as the Proverb tells us to do, she was brought up in the way she should go. But it had not prevented the devil from creeping in and creating havoc in her life, finding her one sensitive point, prodding it unmercifully and flaming her complex into anger and resentment against the God who had so created her.

I am sure that, as we had done, Stephanie's parents had often asked themselves where they had gone wrong. But, like us, they had faithfully continued to pray for their daughter, believing against all odds that God could still bring good out of this terrible evil into which she had fallen.

Had her story been fiction, Stephanie would no doubt have married the young man who had converted her and who had had such a profound influence on her. But truth is stranger than fiction, and the Lord had other plans for her life.

Some time later we met her again in Paris, more radiant than ever, and she introduced us to her husband, 'my Mr Wonderful' as she calls him, a man standing even taller than she.

Stephanie and Dan had met when her brother brought him to spend Christmas at their parents' home. Dan had never been physically in prison but he had spent his youth rebelling against practically everything, and when he entered the warm atmosphere of the Millers' home he had reached the end of his tether and touched the depths of human despair. And it was Stephanie who, through her acceptance of him as he was and her unconditional friendship which slowly turned to love, gave him back his taste for living and led him to accept Jesus as his personal Saviour.

'The Lord has even turned our height to his advantage,' Dan laughed. 'When we walk around a town people turn and stare, then we smile and get into conversation and it's so often proved to be an occasion to share with them what Jesus has done in both our lives.'

Together they have been all over the world ministering to prisoners.

'But it's not only people behind bars, locked in a cell who are prisoners,' Stephanie told us sadly. 'So many of those we meet in the street are "prisoners", locked inside themselves like I once was... It's not only in solitary confinement that people can be so terribly alone.'

Dan and Stephanie left for Eastern Europe just a few days after our last meeting to share their faith with other 'prisoners'; to reveal to those who can only see the sky through prison bars that, like the condemned man in Nassau and the young converted prisoner Etienne told us about, knowing Jesus makes all the difference. For as the Bible tells us, he came to bind up the broken-hearted and to set the captives free.

And that the mountain of God's mercy, as all who have experienced it know, is so much greater than the molehill of our sin.

Chapter 23

WHERE THERE IS HATE

When the pattern of our life slowly began to change, as first a daughter-in-law then a son-in-law were added to our family and grandchildren began to appear, I found myself thinking about the kind of world I would like these grandchildren to be brought into if I had the choice. Possibly the world as it would have been, had the serpent not tempted Eve in the Garden of Eden; the earthly paradise God intended for us to inhabit.

And my mind went back to that rainy summer afternoon so many years before when Yves and Christopher had unconsciously made the prophetic statement that 'by getting the man right, the world had come right'. And I realised that we hadn't found any solution, that the world was no nearer being 'put to rights', on the way to becoming once again the Garden of Eden, than it had been then.

The children were all almost grown up. Yves, our long-haired rebel, was now a hard-working young man totally and successfully immersed in his studies at the Sorbonne in Paris but, apart from his complete roundabout turn, in the outside world nothing much had changed.

I longed for a world where our grandchildren could grow up strong and serene, with a purpose and without fear; where I would only hear the tinkle of their laughter and not the screeching of brakes as metal crashed against metal. A world where materialism and humanism had given way to a simple faith and trust in Jesus, where people mattered more than things, where rumours of war were ancient history and where the church had ceased to be a cold, uninviting structure and become a vital, living force. A world where all can walk confidently knowing that they are children of God and have a right to be here; a world in which love your neighbour as yourself is not a theory but reality; a world in which love, compassion, patience, not hate, violence, destruction, greed and deceit are the norm.

An utopia?

No, the pattern for daily living given us by our Lord Jesus Christ.

And as I thought about this I realised that it was no good my raging against the government, the sects, the 'world'. THAT wouldn't get me anywhere.

Jesus had begun with twelve untrained, undisciplined and mostly uneducated men and, with this unlikely material, he had transformed the face of the universe. The ball had to start rolling somewhere, and why not with me? The time I was wasting blaming the present situation on other people was fruitless: the task, anyway, was hopeless if one looked at it from one's own position, but the Bible says 'nothing is impossible with God'. He asks us to stretch out in love there where we are and, if each one of us who knows him pledged to do just this here and now, it wouldn't take long to change the face of today's world. And we could end up with a universe where Jesus Christ is Lord and King.

As we turn the pages of the New Testament we see leaping out at us the cure for all this tired world's ills: it is in that unconditional, agape love which seeks not so much to be loved as to love, asking nothing in return. That love which gives a meaning to life, a framework for daily living, where children are taught to respect their parents and parents told not to provoke their children. Where honour thy father and thy mother means that there is no longer loneliness and heartache in old age. That love which teaches that there is no special merit in loving the lovable, but where love your enemies is the rule rather than the exception. That love which would empty the psychiatric wards because it washes away all guilt, forgives every sin and turns the page to a new life, as it says in the book of Isaiah:

> Forget the former things, do not dwell on the past. See, I am doing a new thing! Now it springs up. Do you not perceive it?

A boundless love without any strings attached, offered freely to all who will accept it and be born again to a new life and a daily walk with Jesus, secure because he has promised that nothing, ever, can separate us from his love, not even death. And our life in his hands is the ultimate secret of peace.

And as these thoughts raced through my head my prayer was: 'Lord, free all people from the fear of each other, that fear which leads us to trust in force and violence instead of in you. Pour into us your love, that love whose ultimate purpose is to overflow and not to be greedily hoarded. Take away all selfish pride and help us to realise that people don't care how much we know until they know how much we care. And lead us to justice and peace.'

As St Francis of Assisi prayed nearly eight hundred years ago:

> Lord make me an instrument of thy peace,
> Where there is hate that I may bring love
> Where there is offence that I may bring pardon
> Where there is discord that I may bring union
> Where there is error that I may bring truth
> Where there is doubt that I may bring faith
> Where there is despair that I may bring hope
> Where there is darkness that I may bring light
> Where there is sadness that I may bring joy.
> O Master, make me not so much to be consoled

as to console; not so much to be loved as to love;
not so much to be understood as to understand;
for it is in giving that one receives;
it is in self-forgetfulness that one finds;
it is in pardoning that one is pardoned;
it is in dying that one finds eternal life.

Chapter 24

IMMORTALITY

Shortly after my first book was published I was asked to speak at a luncheon, and when question time came a lady seated at the back of the room stood up.

'Are you writing another book?'

'I haven't any plans to write one for the time being,' I replied.

'Why not?' my questioner pursued.

'I'm afraid I'm too busy with other things,' I smiled, thinking the matter would end there.

But it didn't.

'What are you doing?' she went on.

'Well,' I hesitated, not quite sure just what was filling all my time, 'I'm rather taken up with our grandchildren.'

Hervé and Bee had spent the first four years of married life in Morocco and when they returned Bee began working as a part-time secretary to her eldest brother, Olivier, who had set up his office in a guest house we had in the garden. When their baby daughter arrived I offered to look after her whilst Bee was in the office.

I loved looking after that baby girl and Yves and Christopher, her young uncles, who were still living at home at that time, adored her. It was an ideal arrangement all round. Bee gave me Margaux when she arrived in the morning, often popped in and had lunch with us and a cuddle with her daughter and, should there be a problem, I merely had to cross the garden to ask her advice.

Our second son, also called Hervé like Bee's husband, and his wife had, after spending the whole of their married life either abroad or in the provinces, finally came to live very near us. And, Cécile, our daughter-in-law, told us how much it meant to their three little girls to at last live near grandparents, be able to pop in, and to have the security of a 'second home', as I had had at Great-Aunt Jessica's.

It was wonderful. We saw a lot of all four granddaughters, but I was no longer twenty and found that my energy didn't run, at the end of the day, to writing books as well!

But my questioner was not satisfied with my answer.

'You're wrong,' rang out from her place at the back of the hall. 'God has given us all gifts and he means us to use them!'

I had no reply to this and her statement bothered me, until I took my problem to the Lord in prayer.

'Am I wrong?' I asked Jesus one morning, not long afterwards. 'Should I try to write another book and find some other arrangement for baby Margaux?'

The Lord did not answer me immediately, but when the answer did come it was surprising, and humiliating.

But it gave me peace.

'If you are really writing for me,' Jesus said quietly, 'I will find you the time.'

He paused and I felt his eyes upon me.

'But if you are wanting to write the book for you...'

It was clear in my mind what my Lord meant, but I wasn't ready to acknowledge it yet.

'The pursuit of success, popularity or status is a very dangerous road for the Christian to take,' Jesus went on. 'My Holy Spirit dwells within you so that I might shine forth, not so that you may be a showpiece. Only the success which brings glory to God must be allowed to motivate your life.'

I dared not raise my eyes.

'Be like the musician playing with the orchestra,' Jesus continued. 'He does not need the praise of the audience if he can only catch the look of approval from his master. Your worth to God in public depends on what you are to him in private, not on the adulation of the world.'

In the stillness, I could almost feel his eyes looking right through me.

'In ten years time will anyone even remember that you have written a book?' Jesus asked.

I bit my lip. I didn't know.

'But what you do for those little girls,' he said kindly, 'will live on. You are helping to shape the minds and the thought patterns of the next generation and because of what you are teaching them now, their children and perhaps even their grandchildren will be affected. That is where you will be remembered.'

He paused.

'The Bible says that the sins of the fathers will be visited upon their children unto the third and fourth generation,' Jesus went on.

I nodded.

'Not only the sins,' he said softly, 'but also the good, the influence which you pass on.'

The silence in the room was total.

'Remember Great-Aunt Jessica?' he ended.

I caught my breath as I realised that the wheel had turned full circle and that the little girl who, more than fifty years earlier, had run with her joys and her tears, her difficulties and her questions to Great-Aunt Jessica was now herself standing in her Great-Aunt's place. I was now the older generation, part of the solid wall which formed the framework of our family, giving love and security not only to our own children but to their children as well.

And it was in that moment that, for the first time, I fully understood the immensity of God's love. I realised that there is no time when he begins to love us, he has always loved us and that every human being, every child born in his image is unique and of value in his eyes. God could have created the universe without me, without these precious grandchildren, but he didn't. He didn't WANT a universe without them, without Jacques, without our children or without all those members of our family who had gone before because as the Bible tells us, he loves us with an everlasting love.

As these thoughts flooded through my mind and Jesus's words sank, in the dawn broke in my subconscious and revealed to me to that happiness is not a smooth road to travel or success, or even the successful doing of a thing, but knowing the perfect fulfilment of that for which we were created.

We all have to find our niche in life, that task for which we have been specially created and, spiritually, I think we find it when we receive our personal ministry from the Lord. And in that moment I knew without any shadow of a doubt that God had created me first and foremost a mother.

It was as if a bright light had suddenly been switched on, illuminating the hidden corners of my mind and, as I felt a great peace and joy surge through me, I could only praise and worship my Saviour in that special heavenly language he had put into my mouth so many years before.

Human words seemed too trite; there weren't any which could express the immense love and gratitude which longed to reach out to Jesus at that very moment. I felt like a surf rider bouncing over the waves, and as the unknown words ended I suddenly heard my voice raised in a beautiful song of praise, soaring, gliding, dipping and finally gracefully landing as the words ceased.

But then, before I had time to take another breath, the same tune sprang from my lips again, only this time the words which flowed out were in English, glorious, thrilling, beautiful verse, perfect in structure and cadence, a poem I could never have written, a heavenly hymn of worship and adoration to him who alone is worthy of our praise.

It was one of those rare moments God gives us in the midst of our everyday life, another hilltop experience. Mostly our walk is everyday living, often drudgery but, just occasionally, and I don't believe we are to expect it as our due, Jesus gives us an extra bonus, a thrill, and this is what he did for me that morning.

I saw the sea and the waves which had distressed me, in which I had been struggling, trying to swim against the frothing surf, uncertain, undecided, questioning. And suddenly all my doubts about the rightness of what I was doing vanished as the Lord took me and, like a surf-rider, bounced me triumphantly through the foam. I rose above it, was on top of it, dominating it, using it instead of allowing it to submerge me: feeling the wind in my hair, the tang of salt on my lips, singing my way through it where before I had felt breathless and weary with the effort.

Jesus was showing me that when we are in his perfect will we are more than conquerors, we don't have to fight the difficult and puzzling situations which crop up in our lives, we merely have to hand the problem over to him because he has already won the battle for us.

'Go now,' Jesus said quietly, as the experience faded and my words of praise ceased 'and continue to do my work with these children. When the time comes, I will give you another book.'

As I rose from my knees I simply didn't care whether I would ever write another book or not. I was so satisfied, so fulfilled, so at peace knowing that I was in his perfect will, doing just what he wanted me to do with my life ... at that point in time.

Chapter 25

HIS AWESOME LOVE

As I look back over the years I realise what a lot of time I have wasted facing disasters in my mind which God never meant me to face and which, in reality, I was never called upon to face. And what a sin it is to worry when we have put our whole trust in him and our hand in the hand of Jesus.

On that memorable morning when I once again sought his will for my life Jesus pointed out to me that our thought pattern forms the thought pattern of the next generation – those who look to us for guidance. We can be an influence for good or for evil, for positive or for negative thinking, for worry or for peace of mind, and it was humbling to realise what a responsibility is ours as women in the home, not only towards our own families but towards the future of the whole world.

My years as a mother, almost half my life, have taught me that in order to develop normally, to blossom, children need more than anything else to believe that the world is a friendly place, that there are people in it who are trustworthy, that their place in it is secure and that they can, when the time comes, make their own way in it.

And this they can only do if the foundations, their personal foundations, are right; if we have built those foundations firmly with Jesus as the cornerstone and instilled in our children a positive attitude. Like Jesus, children see straight into our hearts, straight through us to the beauty or the camouflage beneath, and it is not what we say which will affect or impress them, nor what we do. It is what we are.

We are told to 'walk in the light as he is in the light', to 'put aside the deeds of darkness and put on the armour of light', his armour which is utterly transparent and yet protects us and keeps us from those powers of darkness.

As children of God we are only of use to him and to our children if our lives are able to stand up under close scrutiny and are transparent, so that our 'inside' life reflects on the 'outside' and we don't just have a religious veneer, be white-washed tombs as the Pharisees were. For Jesus sees us as we really are. He does not see us as other people see us, or even as we see ourselves, and he is the only one who is able to 'turn on our inner light' – without him we remain children of darkness.

As I thought about this, I realised that in the days before the electronic age the way a bank cashier detected a false note was by holding it up to the light. By merely handling it or rustling it through his fingers he could not tell the genuine from the false, they both looked alike. But once held up to the light, the bank note which was false was immediately detected.

It is rather like our lives.

We too can be very good imitations, until we are held up to the light. Or we can be so close to Jesus, so identified with him, so much one with him that we are not afraid to be held up to the light, because we know that only Jesus will shine through.

Sadly, we haven't created for our children the perfect world, the land fit for heroes which we all idyllically imagined would result from the last war nor, I fear, have we fought the war to end all wars.

But as I look around at my little brood, in spite of the rumbles and tensions and threats which hang over our planet, in spite of the heartaches and the agonising over them in the night which Jacques and I have gone through over the years, it has been worth it to see them all now 'launched'.

None of us knows what tomorrow will bring but, for the moment at least, their lives seem to be happy and fulfilled and, what is very precious and important in our eyes, we have kept them in the circle of our love – and they still enjoy the family occasions when they are all together in their 'old home'.

But I know I could not have guided them through without Jesus, without the knowledge that even in our darkest hour we can before, not as escapists but as the world's only true realists because he has rescued us from the power of darkness. For Jesus said: 'I am the light of the world. Whoever follows me will never walk in darkness but will have the light of life.'

And also perhaps, from an earthly point of view, without the meaning of Great-Aunt Jessica, for I see now what a tremendous influence she had on my life, how her standards and principles had become embedded in me without my even noticing it.

I don't think she consciously strove to 'educate' me or to bring me up, she was far too discreet to interfere, but she was always there and she took it as her duty to be a bulwark and a haven, not only for her younger sisters, but also for their children and grandchildren. And, in doing so, without ever realising it or even striving to attain it, she has achieved 'immortality' in this world, as those values and principles which she lived by and passed on to me, I tried to pass on to my own children. Now, perhaps without their even realising it either, they in their turn are passing them on to their children.

Mother Teresa once said: 'We must make our homes centres of love and compassion and forgive endlessly.'

And Great-Aunt Jessica, strict and Victorian as she was, did just that. The relationship I had with her coloured and formed the relationship I later came to know with God – not in the early part of my Christian walk, but as I went deeper into this wonderful new life we have when we meet Jesus, my relationship with him subtly changed.

In the beginning I had been so overwhelmed by the joy, the

beauty, the breathlessness of being his child and having this special link with my Creator, that I think I tended at times to forget that he WAS my Creator and didn't give him the respect and reverence he deserved. It was a chummy union at first, we were on first name terms, but as I went deeper into my life with him I understood that that was not what God wanted of me, his child. Looking back to my relationship with Great-Aunt Jessica helped me to adjust my relationship with my Saviour.

I loved my Great-Aunt, I admired her and I knew I could trust her completely in all situations, but I also had profound respect for her and was a little in awe of her. We didn't relate on a 'chummy' basis at all. It would never have occurred to any of us to be so familiar as to call her Jessie or Jess as perhaps today's young people might have done, and anyway she would never have allowed it. Nor would I have dreamt of disobeying or contradicting, even arguing with her, although as in the case of Geraldine's appalling 'greed' I knew I could take my grievances to her for arbitration, and that she would quietly but firmly mete out justice and put things right.

And that is how I now feel about God. Complete, utter trust, devotion and love, but also reverence and tremendous awe in the face of his power and might and majesty. The chummy days have gone and I now stand and gaze at the wonderful things he has done, not only in my own life but in the whole of creation. I know I cannot begin to fathom the depth of his love and the greatness of his majesty, and with this knowledge comes the conviction that, in my finite state and perhaps one day even in my infinite state, I can never be on nickname terms with one who is clothed in such glory.

It isn't that I love him less. On the contrary, I love him even more. I didn't love Great-Aunt Jessica less because I would never have dreamt of answering her back or questioning her authority, and in the same way and for the same reasons I don't love God less because I now stand in awe before him.

I think I explained this feeling, to a lesser degree, once to

Christopher when he did something of which I disapproved and I told him so in no uncertain terms. He looked at me in astonishment. I have never been much of a sergeant major in the home and I'm afraid the childrens' upbringing has been rather easygoing so he was obviously taken aback to hear me react so strongly.

'I thought you were my friend,' he said in surprise.

'I AM your friend,' I replied, the tension of the moment gone, 'but I am first and foremost your mother.'

My statement appeared to baffle him.

'You have dozens of friends,' I smiled, 'but you have only one mother.'

And that sums up my relationship with Jesus.

He is my friend, and I have many friends; but he is first and foremost my God. And I have only one God. As such he demands not only my love and adoration but also my reverence and, above all, my awe.

And I wonder if that sense of awe and reverence, which does not in any way exclude love and complete trust, but rather enhances it, is what is sometimes missing in contemporary Christianity.

Chapter 26

THE END OF AN ERA

As long as Great-Aunt Jessica was alive, the cousins and second cousins still had that invisible thread which linked them together, but when she died the thread weakened and finally broke. They were a strong, upright generation, those mid-Victorians, and Aunt Jessica and her sisters must have been particularly tough to have survived as long as they did.

It was strange that my grandmother, the 'delicate' one, was the last to go. She who had always hated to be alone, and could never have contemplated living alone, saw her brother and all her sisters leave this earth before her.

Great-Aunt Gwendolen died, I think, of a broken heart. The war had taken both her husband and her only son and, although she remained as dignified as ever and would never have admitted her pain or given in to self-pity, when Geraldine left for Kenya the spark seemed to go out of her.

Great-Aunt Julia, whom we didn't see so often as she lived in the north of Scotland, was the next, carried to her Highland grave by her six stalwart sons.

When Uncle Fergus died of a sudden heart attack, Great-Aunt Prudence barricaded herself in the house with his body and had to be forcibly removed. She did not survive her beloved husband for long and died shortly after him, a bewildered, pathetic but still very beautiful woman, lost in a world of her own not able, or perhaps not wanting, to recognise any member of her family.

Great-Uncle Cecil died as he had lived, convinced he was a failure. To everyone's astonishment he had married his maid when well into middle age and produced Ronnie, a severely handicapped son. When Ronnie reached school age he was pushed around, drooling and vacant, in what was then called a bathchair, wearing a blazer with a schoolboy cap perched on his lolling head in a pathetic attempt by his mother to pretend that there was nothing wrong.

Ronnie died in his early teens and Great-Aunt Maggie was taken ill with pneumonia, which before the war was often fatal, and laid to rest beside her son shortly afterwards. I think when Ronnie died she no longer had any wish to live, as it must have been as obvious to her as it was to everyone else that her marriage to Uncle Cecil had been a dreadful mistake.

After his wife's death, Great-Uncle Cecil slipped back into his old life almost as if the whole incident had never occurred and the only tangible reminder of this ill-fated union to remain was Grace, who couldn't have been more unfortunately named. She was a middle-aged, highly capable nurse with a shaggy fringe, thick pebble glasses and very prominent teeth who had been appointed to look after Ronnie.

Grace had been devoted to her unresponsive charge and when Uncle Cecil was finally alone again she just stayed on, bustling briskly about the house when she wasn't driving around in the pony and trap, which had been bought in an attempt to awaken a spark of interest in Ronnie's glazed eyes.

I only met Ronnie once or twice and no one ever explained his illness to me. It was always just glossed over, but I remember being terribly afraid of this tall gangling youth who flopped when put in an upright position and was unable to walk unaided.

But I loved and admired Grace and longed to have 'sticky-out' teeth, as I called them, like she did. In fact, I spent a great deal of time in front of my bedroom mirror as a child attempting to force my top teeth into an almost horizontal position and, when I realised that this was getting me nowhere, I tried to remember to open my mouth and rest them on my bottom lip whenever possible.

I well remember my mother looking curiously at me one afternoon at tea.

'What on *earth* are you doing?' she finally enquired.

It was one of the times when I *had* remembered and was sitting opposite her with my top teeth almost obscuring my chin.

'Trying to look like Grace,' I had replied, and ended with a deep sigh. 'I do wish you were as beautiful as she is.'

I don't think my mother was all that pleased.

But children do sometimes have strange ideas and my remark that afternoon certainly illustrated the proverb: 'beauty is in the eye of the beholder'. Grace was certainly not beautiful in any way, on the outside, but like our Lord I had obviously seen beyond her ugly exterior to the beauty which lay hidden beneath.

She stayed with Uncle Cecil right to the end, transferring all the love and devotion she had showered on Ronnie on to him. But I wonder whether he even noticed she was still around.

Great-Uncle Cecil didn't appear to die at all, he just wasn't there one day and, like his life, his death left no trace in the sand. Only Grannie and Grace were left to grieve for him. And I think they both truly did, though Grannie's Victorian upbringing would never have allowed her to show it.

Her younger brother had a special place in her heart right to the end. Perhaps he was the only one who had been able to touch those deep recesses and reveal the tenderness, the love which must have been there, hidden somewhere beneath the layers of autocracy and pride.

Great-Aunt Jessica died at ninety-two, just a few months before Uncle Cecil. One could never imagine her doing anything in an other than dignified way and, as she was in life, so she was in death. She merely sat down in her wing armchair in front of her drawing room fire one winter afternoon after returning from a ladies' working party for the local church bazaar, and peacefully passed away.

She left no heir, no tangible, physical reminder of herself, only a selfless loving legacy of devotion and service to her family which it would be hard to equal. She understood that those who love us let us find our own way and made her service of love a beautiful thing.

When my grandmother was left alone, the last survivor of that incredible family, the grapevine finally stopped working and with her passing a whole era of our lives disappeared.

Grannie's funeral was the last big family gathering, and a photograph taken afterwards more resembled a wedding group than a funeral party. Her four remaining nephews were there but sadly no great nephews. There were only three of Great-Aunt Julia's 'boys' left, and those of their sons who survived the war – for they had all immediately rushed into the most dangerous battle zones – had scattered to various parts of the world.

Sybil's brother, John, who was one of the 'younger' ones, had turned completely white and looked very frail. Maybe his traumatic childhood had prematurely aged him, but he died not long afterwards, having collapsed at the altar after receiving communion from his only child's husband.

Sybil, who had found peace when she found Jesus, had joined the Catholic Church and spent most of her time travelling around Europe. She died in Bavaria, knocked down by a car whilst crossing the road. It was a part of Europe which she had come to love and where she spent most of her time and had many Christian friends. So when my brother went over to attend her funeral, as the only male member of the family available, he said that he thought the crowd which followed Sybil to her foreign grave was infinitely greater than it would have been had she died in her own country, which held only unhappy memories.

When my mother died Geraldine wrote to me from Africa,

and then a few years later she wrote again saying that she and her husband were in the Lake District and would like to come over to France to see us.

It was just before Bee's wedding and I answered, sending them an invitation.

'We won't know anyone,' Geraldine had replied, 'we've never met your husband or your children and it would be easier for you if we came afterwards. I want to see *you* again, and you'll be too busy at such a time.'

I saw what she meant and a week after the wedding I drove to the station to meet this cousin whom I had not seen for over thirty years.

'Will I even recognise her?' I panicked. 'And worse, will we have anything to say to each other?'

I remembered Clive as being very tall and like all tall, lean men stooping slightly and of course, I comforted myself, there are very few redheads in France so I'll recognise Geraldine by that shock of auburn curls.

But it wasn't the Geraldine of almost forty years earlier who was waiting for me, it was a replica of Great-Aunt Gwendolen as I last remembered her: tall, slim, elegant with immaculately dressed white hair.

And I need not have worried, after the first few strained moments when we eyed each other incredulously, each having a vision of the young girls we once had been, the ice broke and almost before we were settled in the garden with tea Geraldine and I had gone back down the years boring everyone with our cries of '. . . and do you remember?' as two ageing ladies collapsed in helpless giggles.

During that week they spent with us we talked and reminisced and I thanked God yet again for ordaining the wonderful institution of a family, for that invisible, strong thread which runs through it and, in spite of time and distance, binds us close one to the other, if only we will let it.

'We're the only ones left now, apart from Geoffrey, Tom and Brian,' Geraldine said quietly on their last morning, when we were sitting alone together in the garden, our giggling fits over.

It didn't seem possible that out of that web of tangled relationships into which we had been in those years before the war, the cousins who had squabbled and laughed and played together at Great-Aunt Jessica's, the aunts, the uncles, we five should be the only ones left. And yet we were.

And I realised then how quickly life passes, what a short span of time we spend on this earth. As the Bible says, man is like a blade of grass, here today and gone tomorrow. And how urgent is the message which we have to pass on to those who come after us, and especially to those who are our precious responsibility... our children.

Herbert Hoover once said cynically, 'Blessed are the young for they shall inherit the national debt.'

As Geraldine and I sat under the trees among the roses and the twittering birdsong that warm June morning, I thought how very sad if that is all we have to leave them in this age when so many wonderful things have happened that the mind boggles.

As Christians we know that one day all our questions will be answered, all the creases in our understanding ironed out, all our problems solved when we come face to face with our Creator and, at last, understand this great mystery of God become man.

But as parents here and now, caring Christian parents who love and respect God's Word, I am convinced that the one thing of worth, apart from a strong enduring bond of family love, which we can leave our children in the midst of this present doubt and confusion is this: our positive joyful conviction, our deep assurance that, more important than all the scientific feats which this century has produced, feats which would have been science fiction to my grandmother, more important even than the fact that in 1969 man accomplished the unbelievable and walked on the moon, is the knowledge that, almost two thousand years before, an event which is even more unbelievable occurred, when Jesus Christ the Son of God became man and walked on the earth, putting eternity within the reach of us all. And he is still alive and walking with us today offering us ... only the best. All we have to do is reach out to him and accept it.

We will tell the next generation the praiseworthy deeds of the Lord, his power and the wonders he has done ... so that the next generation would know them, even the children yet to be born, and they in turn would tell their children. Then they would put their trust in God. (Psalm 78:4,6,7).

ABORTION: A WOMAN'S BIRTHRIGHT?

Noreen Riols

Noreen Riols was happily married with four children, but the birth of the fifth plunged her into an unexpected and dark world of depression. A breakdown confined her to a mental hospital for six months before life seemed manageable again. Then, when she became pregnant once more, the advice was clear: have an abortion.

The decision was agonising but there seemed no choice. Only when Noreen accepts the love and forgiveness of God can she forgive herself and find real healing.

'Few people who have had an abortion have the courage or ability to express the long-term effects that this has had on them as individuals. Noreen Riols writes sensitively and movingly. This book should be widely read.'

Anne Townsend, Care Trust

EYE OF THE STORM

Noreen Riols

Noreen Riols' life was in shreds. Living in Paris with her French husband and struggling to cope with five children, she could not counter the black despair that dragged her into a nervous breakdown. At first she didn't believe that the joy in the lives of Christian friends could be hers as well.

Her conversion was immediate and real, but her faith was to be tested in the continuing ups and downs of family life. Seeing the power of God at work in the miraculous healing of her husband, Noreen testifies to a loving God who can make all things new. Her story will charm, move and encourage.

'Here real life experiences, described by a gifted writer, grip the reader better than an exciting novel... but the events actually happened.'

Today magazine

'A very special book. Definitely not to be missed.'

Floodtide

'Superb, well-written, fast-moving, effective, interesting... a book that could be of great help to many Christians who are still on the fringe of true faith.'

BBC Radio Kent